THE ULTIMATE

MEAL PLANNING

FOR ONE

COOKBOOK

Includes 8 weekly meal plans designed for one!

100+ Easy, Affordable, and Low-Waste (High-Taste!) Recipes Made Just for You

Kelly Jaggers, Author of *The Ultimate Mediterranean Diet Cooking for One Cookbook*

Adams Media

New York London Toronto Sydney New Delhi

Adams Media
An Imprint of Simon & Schuster, LLC
100 Technology Center Drive
Stoughton, Massachusetts 02072

First Adams Media trade paperback edition July 2024

ADAMS MEDIA and colophon are registered trademarks of Simon & Schuster, LLC.

Simon & Schuster: Celebrating 100 Years of Publishing in 2024

For information about special discounts for bulk purchases, please contact Simon & Schuster Special Sales at 1-866-506-1949 or business@simonandschuster.com.

The Simon & Schuster Speakers Bureau can bring authors to your live event. For more information or to book an event, contact the Simon & Schuster Speakers Bureau at 1-866-248-3049 or visit our website at www.simonspeakers.com.

Interior design by Kellie Emery
Images © 123RF/Diana Johanna Velasquez, chelovector

Manufactured in the United States of America

1 2024

Library of Congress Cataloging-in-Publication Data
Names: Jaggers, Kelly, author.
Title: The ultimate meal planning for one cookbook / Kelly Jaggers, Author of The Ultimate Mediterranean Diet Cooking for One Cookbook.
Description: First Adams Media trade paperback edition. | Stoughton, Massachusetts: Adams Media, 2024. | Series: Ultimate for one cookbooks series | Includes index.
Identifiers: LCCN 2024007959 | ISBN 9781507222430 (pb) | ISBN 9781507222447 (ebook)
Subjects: LCSH: Cooking for one. | Quick and easy cooking. | Low budget cooking. | Waste minimization. | LCGFT: Cookbooks.
Classification: LCC TX652 .J29 2024 | DDC 641.5/611--dc23/eng/20240304
LC record available at https://lccn.loc.gov/2024007959

ISBN 978-1-5072-2243-0
ISBN 978-1-5072-2244-7 (ebook)

DEDICATION

To my stalwart husband and taste tester, Mark.
I could not do what I do without your support and love.

CONTENTS

INTRODUCTION

Meal planning is an easy way to enjoy your favorite foods while reducing waste and saving money. And when you are also a solo cook, meal planning allows you to focus on the dishes and menus that suit your personal tastes. Of course, planning your meals for the week ahead can feel daunting at first, especially when many recipes out there aren't designed to feed just one person. A recipe that yields six servings is overwhelming for any one cook, not to mention the idea of eating that same meal for another 5 days.

The good news is that *The Ultimate Meal Planning for One Cookbook* is here to help! In this book, you'll find 140 delicious recipes that yield one or two servings each (or more, for some treats and snacks)—perfect for the solo chef. Organized into chapters by course, there are easy and flavorful options for every meal (and meal plan!). For example, on Monday morning, you can make a hearty Ham and Cheddar Breakfast Bake (Chapter 3), which makes another portion to enjoy later in the week. For lunch, you can whip up a batch of creamy Soba Noodles with Peanut Sauce (Chapter 6), which are ready in less than 20 minutes. At snack time, make a perfect-for-one portion of Pimento Cheese Spread (Chapter 4) to pair with whole-grain crackers or celery sticks. For dinner, sweet and tangy Honey Mustard–Roasted Chicken Legs (Chapter 9), which you prepped ahead on Sunday, will be out of the oven just as Saffron Rice (Chapter 5) finishes steaming. For a sweet ending to the day, pull one (or two) portions of Freeze and Bake Chocolate Chip Cookies (Chapter 10) from the freezer for ooey-gooey chocolate chip cookie bliss in less than 15 minutes.

But before you start planning and cooking these recipes, you'll want to look at the first two chapters on meal planning. In Chapter 1, you'll learn more about meal planning itself, including how it differs from meal prepping, what to include on your shopping lists, and tips to make cooking for one a breeze. Then, in Chapter 2, you'll discover eight sample weekly meal plans created with recipes in this book. Each plan is complete with a shopping list and tips for prep you can do to make day-of cooking easier. These plans even factor in going out to eat one or two times each week, so you won't need to worry about missing out on your favorite restaurants or upcoming occasions. Whether you use the plans as written, give them some personal touches, or simply return to them for reference when creating your own plans, you will be able to step into the kitchen with confidence.

When you have delicious recipes and helpful tips and guides on hand, meal planning and cooking for one is easy—and can even be fun! Whether you want to stick to a budget, minimize the time you spend in the kitchen, or indulge in your favorite foods without having mountains of leftovers, *The Ultimate Meal Planning for One Cookbook* is for you. Enjoy!

CHAPTER 1

MEAL PLANNING FOR ONE

Meal planning for one is the process of creating a weekly menu built around your own food preferences and cooking goals using recipes that yield one to two servings each. People choose to meal plan for a variety of reasons. For some, it is a way to ease decision fatigue at the end of a long day, while others plan as a way to prevent food waste and stay on budget. In addition, cooking for one is often faster and easier than cooking from recipes designed to feed four or more, so you can spend less time in the kitchen and more time enjoying your creations! Creating a weekly meal plan for one will help you meet your personal goals—whatever they may be.

This chapter has all the information you need to successfully start meal planning like a pro. You will find tips on how to create crave-worthy weekly meal plans; how to construct a weekly grocery list that includes shopping for your own refrigerator, freezer, and pantry; ways to prep and store foods for the week; and how to prepare ingredients for longer storage. You will also find lists of pantry staples and kitchen tools that will help make planning and cooking throughout the week easier, as well as information about food safety. With all the right information, you will have a solid foundation to start building your meal plans each week and cooking dishes you will love!

Meal Planning versus Meal Prepping

You have likely heard the term "meal prepping" at some point in your experiences with cooking. So what is the difference between meal planning and meal prepping? In meal prepping, you are cooking larger batches of food that are divided into multiple portions to eat throughout the week. For example, when meal prepping, you might be cooking five meals of roasted chicken breast and mixed vegetables on Sunday, dividing them into preportioned containers, and eating those meals Monday through Friday.

With meal planning, you are working out a weekly menu for breakfasts, lunches, snacks, dinners, and desserts that is made up of some single-serving meals and some cook-once, eat-twice options so you can plan for leftovers and don't have to cook every meal every day. The majority of the recipes in this book make no more than two servings, the exceptions being some make-ahead, cook-when-ready-to-eat items like Freeze and Bake Chocolate Chip Cookies (Chapter 10), where you'd only be cooking one serving at a time but might have more servings prepared in advance to cook later. Meal planning offers more variety and flexibility than meal prepping, where you are eating foods that have been batch cooked in advance.

With meal planning, the extent of the "prep work" is preparing ingredients so they're ready or easier to use: You might be marinating meat the day before cooking, cutting lots of vegetables at once to use later in the week, or even mixing the ingredients for entire dishes together and storing them to cook when you want to eat.

How to Create a Meal Plan

Sitting down to create your very first meal plan may feel a little intimidating. Where do you start? What steps do you need to take? This section will walk you through each step for creating a meal plan from start to finish. To help you along, there are also 8 weeks of sample meal plans and shopping and prep lists provided in Chapter 2, which you can use as templates each week or use for the first few weeks while you get comfortable with the process of meal planning for one.

Step One: Planning with Your Schedule in Mind

The best way to start a meal plan is to look at your schedule for the week. Between work and personal activities, there will be days when you have more time to be in the kitchen creating delicious meals and other days when you will need something tasty that takes just a few minutes to get ready. Also note: You may not want to plan every meal each day. For example, if you are not a big breakfast eater or snacker or you do not eat desserts every day, you can skip planning these meals. The beauty of meal planning for one is that you are only taking your needs and desires into consideration. No need to plan for meals or snacks you do not want or enjoy!

With this information, you can decide on the number of meals you will want for the week for breakfasts, lunches, dinners, snacks, and desserts. Look at your weekly schedule and your preferences and make note of the following:

- Which days will you have time to spend in the kitchen?
- Which days will you need faster meals or leftovers?
- Which days will you have plans or not be cooking?

Remember, your meal plan is not inflexible. You can make impromptu plans and simply shift a meal to another day or eliminate it as needed. You can also swap meals from day to day as your cravings change. Your meal plan does not dictate your schedule; your schedule dictates your meal plan.

Step Two: Checking Your Refrigerator, Freezer, and Pantry

Keeping track of the food and supplies you have in your kitchen will help you reduce food waste, keep you from overbuying the same ingredients you already have, and ultimately save you money. It will also make your weekly meal planning faster and easier because you will readily be able to see what items you have on hand. Some people create spreadsheets to track their kitchen inventory, while others use good old pen and paper. Whatever track-

ing strategy you choose, be sure to update your inventory weekly so you know what you have available.

For the first week of meal planning, you will want to create your inventory by sorting through your pantry, freezer, and refrigerator and making a detailed list of what you have and in what quantities. It is also handy to make note of spices you have on hand as well as dry goods like flour, sugar, and other baking staples. Organizing your inventory by category is one of the best ways to keep track of what you have. It can be divided as follows:

- Fresh fruit and vegetables
- Fresh meat
- Fresh dairy and eggs
- Frozen fruit and vegetables
- Frozen meat
- Baking supplies
- Spices and herbs
- Grains and cereals
- Canned goods
- Condiments, dressings, and marinades
- Oil and vinegar

The first inventory will take the longest, but it is worth the investment in time to make your planning fast and easy down the road. This is also an excellent time to toss out any expired, old, or spoiled items and organize your pantry, freezer, and refrigerator so you are starting your meal planning for one journey fresh!

Step Three: Selecting Recipes

Now that you know how many meals (and which kinds of meals) you need for which days, how long you will have to prepare these recipes each day, and what items you have in your kitchen, you can start to select the recipes. The best advice for meal planning for one is this: Pick meals you enjoy and want to eat. The easiest way to stick to a weekly meal plan is to make meals you love! With that in mind, here are a few notes to consider when selecting recipes for the week:

- Select recipes that allow you to utilize the same ingredients—such as meats, vegetables, and dairy—for more than one meal during the week so you have less food to carry over or preserve and store.
- Consider meals made from planned leftovers from recipes that make two portions for lunches and dinners on very busy days.
- Remember to leave yourself the flexibility to make changes to your meal plan as your schedule or cravings change.

These tips will help you narrow things down when you're browsing through recipes provided later in this book as well as any recipes you find online or through recommendations and are considering trying out.

Step Four: Creating a Grocery List

You know your schedule, you have a kitchen inventory, and you have selected your weekly menu. Now it is time to make your grocery list. This list will include any fresh and pantry items you need to create your meals for the week. Here are some tips for creating a grocery list:

- Read each recipe thoroughly and make note of any ingredients you do not have in your inventory, along with the amount needed.
- Check weekly grocery store ads or circulars for sales or specials so you can shop in a budget-friendly way.
- Organize your shopping list with your local grocery store's layout in mind so you can stop in each department one time to maximize efficiency.
- Note items that can be purchased from the bulk section, such as grains, nuts, dried fruit, and seeds, so you can buy them in smaller quantities.
- Consider buying frozen fruits and vegetables, which are picked and frozen at the height of the season and prepared or chopped, so you can use them right away and save time on busy days.

Fresh and Pantry Staples

To further guide you as you make your shopping list, keep in mind that there are some staple items you will want to have on hand at any given time as well as some fresh items that you will want to stock up on from week to week to make cooking easier. These include:

Pantry Staples

- Almond extract
- Baking powder
- Baking soda
- Beans (canned and dried)
- Broth (chicken, seafood, and vegetable)
- Canned vegetables
- Cocoa powder (Dutch processed)
- Confectioners' sugar
- Cornstarch
- Flour (all-purpose)
- Granulated sugar
- Herbs (dried)
  - Dried bay leaf
  - Dried oregano
  - Dried rosemary
  - Dried tarragon
  - Dried thyme
- Honey
- Ketchup
- Light brown sugar
- Lentils (dried)
- Maple syrup
- Nuts and nut butters
- Olive oil
- Pasta (dried)
- Pickles
- Polenta (dried)
- Pure vanilla extract
- Rice
- Rolled oats
- Vegetable oil
- Vinegar

Freezer Items

- Frozen chicken
- Frozen fruit
- Frozen mussels
- Frozen shrimp
- Frozen vegetables
- Frozen whitefish

Spices (Dried and Ground)

- Cayenne pepper
- Chili powder
- Crushed red pepper flakes
- Freshly cracked black pepper
- Garlic powder
- Ground cinnamon
- Ground cloves
- Ground coriander
- Ground cumin
- Ground fennel
- Ground ginger
- Ground nutmeg
- Onion powder
- Paprika
- Salt
- Sea salt
- Smoked paprika
- Sweet paprika

Dairy

- Butter (salted and unsalted)
- Cheddar cheese (block or shredded)
- Greek yogurt (2% and full-fat)
- Milk (whole or 2%, or alternative dairy-free milk)
- Parmesan cheese (grated)
- Ricotta cheese (whole or part-skim)

Fresh Proteins

- Eggs

Fresh Produce

- Apples
- Asparagus
- Avocados
- Bananas
- Berries
- Carrots
- Citrus fruit
- Cucumbers
- Garlic
- Green onions
- Lettuce
- Mushrooms
- Onions
- Potatoes
- Sweet potatoes
- Tomatoes
- Zucchini

It may help to create a shopping template in a spreadsheet or other tracking app so each week you can easily plug in the ingredients you need to purchase. This way you can also save previous shopping lists and quickly copy them if you are re-creating favorite weekly meal plans, and you can look back on previous shopping trips to see how long ago an item was purchased and estimate when you'll need to restock it.

Step Five: Shopping, Prepping, and Storing

It's the final step of the meal planning for one process! You have your list, and you are ready to get shopping and get your items ready for the week ahead. It is important to stick to your shopping list and avoid impulse purchases, which can lead to overspending and food waste. When you shop, try to shop the perimeter of the store first, where the fresher items are sold, then shop the center section to find dry goods, pastas, canned items, and other grains and spices.

From your shopping list, you will know what ingredients and quantities you need and when it makes sense to stick to those amounts. Cooking for one means you often buy ingredients in smaller quantities, but sometimes items sold in larger quantities have better prices. For example, a two-pack of chicken breasts may be less cost-effective than the family pack of six chicken breasts. It makes more sense to buy the bigger pack at the better price even though it is more than you need. Do not hesitate to take advantage of sales for items like meat, seafood, firm cheese, vegetables, and grains, as they can easily be prepared for longer storage.

Preparing your ingredients before storing them is another great habit to get into when meal planning. Not only will it make cooking easier, but it will also help you avoid stress around timing. After all, timing is important, and you can easily overcook one ingredient because you are busy chopping the next! Take a few minutes to wash and chop the vegetables you will be using for the week and store them in airtight containers in your refrigerator or freezer (more on storage later in this section) so you can measure out what you need as you cook. Meats used in the first few days of your meal plan can be seasoned or marinated—and cut, if required—before storage. Avoid seasoning meat more than 3 days in advance of cooking, however, as it can change the texture of the meat and dry it out. Additionally, be sure to follow safety recommendations when prepping so you can ensure your food stays fresh and safe. These include:

- Washing vegetables and fruits
- Using separate cutting boards, bowls, and containers for raw meat, fish, and seafood to avoid cross contamination with uncooked foods
- Cleaning your counters and any needed appliances before and after preparing food, using a recommended kitchen disinfectant
- Washing your hands with warm soapy water before, during, and after prep, especially after handling raw meat, fish, and seafood and raw flour

Once you've done the shopping and prepping, you'll want to store your ingredients to maximize their shelf life. Here are some tips to make sure your food stays fresh and is stored safely.

Tips for Refrigerating

- Keep fresh meats and fish on the lowest shelf in the coldest part of your refrigerator. Place them on a plate or in a leakproof container to avoid any leaks or runoff.
- Store fresh fruit, vegetables, and salad greens in airtight containers in the refrigerator with paper towels to absorb excess moisture.

- Store washed-and-chopped root vegetables like onions, carrots, and celery in the produce drawer of the refrigerator in a resealable bag or container for up to 1 week.
- Double wrap fresh block cheeses in wax or parchment paper and then store them in the coldest part of the refrigerator to prevent them from drying out or developing mold.
- Store any leftovers in the refrigerator within 30 minutes of cooking and reheat leftovers to an internal temperature of 165°F or until leftovers are hot and steamy.

Tips for Freezing

- Vacuum seal meat in individual portions or wrap in freezer paper or plastic wrap and store in an airtight container. (Will stay fresh for up to 3 months, depending on the meat being stored.)
- Freeze extra vegetables in airtight bags so you can easily measure out what you need for future recipes. (Will stay fresh for up to 3 months.)
- Freeze grains, rice, beans, and flour in airtight bags or containers. (Will last for up to 1 year.)
- Freeze block and shredded firm cheeses like Cheddar, Parmesan, and Swiss wrapped in plastic wrap and stored in a freezer bag. (Will last for up to 8 months. Avoid freezing creamy cheeses like Brie, ricotta, and cream cheese.)

Additional Storage and Safety Tips

- Label ingredients you plan to store with the name of the item and date purchased and add these items to your inventory.
- Store dry goods like flour, oats, and other grains in airtight containers in a dry, dark place at room temperature. (Will last for up to 6 months.)

Using all these tips for shopping, prepping, and safely storing your ingredients will set you up for success as you jump into the next part of meal planning: cooking those tasty recipes for one!

How to Cook for One

Cooking for one is generally easier, faster, and less messy than cooking larger recipes, but there are a few special considerations that will make it even easier and faster! This section covers different aspects of cooking for one, such as how scaled-down recipes cook differently and what additional tools you need to be successful.

Key Differences in Cooking for One

Recipes for one use fewer ingredients than recipes that feed four or more, and smaller quantities mean less prep work. You will spend less time chopping, grating, and generally preparing ingredients since you will be using less for each recipe. You will also do less washing up as you will usually be using fewer bowls, dishes, and other equipment.

Another difference to be aware of is cooking times. Smaller pots and pans with smaller quantities mean quicker cooking times for most recipes. When you are using a smaller pan, it will heat a bit more quickly, and baked items that use smaller pans generally cook more quickly. It is important to use the right-sized pans when cooking for one. Larger pans can cause smaller-quantity recipes to quickly become dry, overcooked, and even burned. You'll explore this more later in this chapter and find a helpful list of pan sizes and other cooking accessories to have on hand when cooking for one.

Tips for Success

The most important way to ensure success in the kitchen is to read the recipe from start to finish before you begin cooking. When you read through, make note of ingredients that are divided and used at different points in the recipe. Be sure to preheat the oven in advance, if called for, and have the right-sized pots and pans cleaned and ready for use. Also, make note of ingredients that need to come to room temperature before cooking so you can have them ready. You should also have all your tools available and prepared per the recipe's instructions so you are not scrambling to find the right spatula or pan during cooking.

Finally, take your time with cooking. Rushing will inevitably lead to mistakes or missed steps. Cooking for one may be easier and faster in general, but that does not mean you should forgo savoring the time spent making a delicious meal! Reread each step of the recipe as you go and pay attention to cooking times as well as how the food looks and smells as you prepare it. Appliances may vary in how they heat, so watch foods that are sautéed or simmered and adjust the heat as needed. For the oven, invest in an oven thermometer to check that it is heating to the proper temperature so your baked goods come out right every time. These small steps will help make your cooking and baking more successful.

Kitchen Tools

As mentioned previously in this chapter, when you are cooking for one, you need to have the right-sized pots, pans, and tools. Cooking with smaller pots, pans, and dishes will ensure your recipes work as they should. Using pots and dishes that are too large will affect cooking times and potentially result in dishes that are overcooked, dry, or unappetizing. The following is a list of the basic pots, pans, dishes, and other kitchen tools used to make the recipes in this book. You may already have some of these in your kitchen, and anything you are missing can be purchased in most home goods retailers or online.

- ¼ rimmed sheet pan
- ½ rimmed sheet pan
- 1-quart saucepan with lid
- 1-quart baking dish
- 2-quart saucepan with lid
- 6" baking or au gratin dish
- 5" × 3" mini-loaf pan
- Six-cup muffin pan
- 2 (4" × 2") cake pans
- 6" pie dish
- 8" ovenproof skillet with lid
- 8" nonstick skillet
- 9" × 5" loaf pan
- Baking parchment or silicone baking mats
- Blender
- Chef's knife
- Cooling rack
- Digital instant-read thermometer
- Digital scale
- Hand mixer
- Measuring cups
- Measuring spoons
- Mixing bowls
- Paring knife
- Serrated knife
- Silicone or rubber spatula
- Spatula
- Tongs
- Whisk
- Wooden spoons

Preparing to Cook for One

Armed with the basics of cooking and meal planning for one as well as the ingredients and tools now stocked in your kitchen, you're ready to start cooking! But before diving in, be sure to check out the next chapter for examples of meal plans. These will be your guide in crafting weekly plans that you can be excited about.

CHAPTER 2

SAMPLE MEAL PLANS

Meal planning for one can seem like a challenge if you have never done it before, but with a bit of guidance, it is a snap! This chapter has 8 weeks of sample meal plans, shopping lists, and suggested optional prep to get you off to a good start. These meal plans are examples that you can follow for your first weeks of planning or that you can use as suggestions for creating your own plans. Be sure to check your pantry, refrigerator, and freezer before shopping with the corresponding grocery lists to ensure you do not already have the ingredients on hand. Also, be sure to read the ingredient lists for the recipes to be sure you have the spices and pantry staples required. Take time to review the optional prep lists as well; these can be easily adapted for your own unique meal plans.

These plans are set up to use as much of the purchased groceries as possible over 1–2 weeks. They note if a recipe makes more than one portion and later where that second portion is used that week or in the week that follows. If you have leftover fresh meat and produce, it is best to freeze them for later use. Some days on the meal plans also note the option of eating out. If you choose to do this, you will want to revise the corresponding grocery list to cut the ingredients needed for the meals listed on those dates. With these samples as your guide, you can easily start developing your own custom meal plans!

WEEK 1: MEAL PLAN

	Breakfast	Lunch	Snack	Dinner	Dessert
Sunday	Ham and Cheddar Breakfast Bake*	Creamy Asparagus Soup	Pimento Cheese Spread	Coconut Curry Shrimp Saffron Rice	Freeze and Bake Chocolate Chip Cookies*
Monday	Ham and Cheddar Scones*	Italian Rotini Salad*	Chunky Guacamole	Honey Mustard– Roasted Chicken Legs Traditional Potato Salad*	Freeze and Bake Chocolate Chip Cookies**
Tuesday	Ham and Cheddar Breakfast Bake**	Chickpea Masala* Saffron Rice	Pimento Cheese Spread	Creamy Smoked Salmon Pasta or Dine Out	Mixed-Berry Crumble
Wednesday	Peach, Granola, and Yogurt Breakfast Parfait	Italian Rotini Salad**	Creamy Fruit Dip*	Summer Vegetable Flatbread	Chocolate Mug Cake
Thursday	Loaded Avocado Toast with Smoked Salmon	Peach-Glazed Pork Chop* Traditional Potato Salad**	Creamy Fruit Dip**	Ravioli Lasagna*	Lemon Blueberry Pound Cake*
Friday	Ham and Cheddar Scones**	Chickpea Masala** Saffron Rice	Chunky Guacamole	Peach-Glazed Pork Chop** Roasted Asparagus with Lemon and Parmesan	Lemon Blueberry Pound Cake**
Saturday	Fluffy Buttermilk Pancakes with Bourbon Maple Syrup	Ravioli Lasagna**	Toasted Ravioli	Braised Beef Short Rib Whipped Yukon Gold Potato with Chives or Dine Out	Fresh Peach Cupcakes* (freeze 3 cupcakes)

*Prep-Ahead Recipe

**Planned Leftovers

WEEK 1: *Shopping List*

Deli
- ☐ 8 ounces Canadian bacon
- ☐ 1 (8-ounce) wedge Parmesan cheese

Bakery
- ☐ 1 loaf whole-grain bread

Meat and Seafood
- ☐ 1 (8-ounce) package smoked salmon
- ☐ 1 (8-ounce) bone-in English beef short rib
- ☐ 2 (6-ounce) boneless pork chops
- ☐ 2 (4-ounce) chicken legs

Produce
- ☐ 2 bunches asparagus
- ☐ 2 large avocados
- ☐ 1 medium lemon
- ☐ 1 medium lime
- ☐ 3 medium peaches
- ☐ 1 small red onion
- ☐ 1 (6-ounce) russet potato
- ☐ 1 (6-ounce) Yukon Gold potato
- ☐ 1 (6-ounce) container fresh blueberries
- ☐ 1 (0.5-ounce) container fresh basil
- ☐ 1 medium zucchini
- ☐ 1 bunch celery
- ☐ 1 (12-ounce) container cherry tomatoes
- ☐ 1 English cucumber
- ☐ 1 bunch fresh cilantro
- ☐ 1 (about 2") piece fresh ginger
- ☐ 2 small yellow onions
- ☐ 1 bulb garlic
- ☐ 1 (16-ounce) container fresh strawberries
- ☐ 1 medium Roma tomato
- ☐ 1 medium red bell pepper

Baking Needs
- ☐ 1 (12-ounce) bag semisweet chocolate chips
- ☐ 1 (1.75-ounce) jar Italian seasoning
- ☐ 1 (1.8-ounce) jar garam masala
- ☐ 1 (3.4-ounce) jar Montreal steak seasoning
- ☐ 1 (2.3-ounce) jar everything bagel seasoning
- ☐ 1 (2-ounce) container dried mustard powder
- ☐ 1 (0.35-ounce) jar freeze-dried dill
- ☐ 1 (0.35-ounce) jar freeze-dried chives
- ☐ 1 (0.06-ounce) jar saffron

Freezer
- ☐ 1 (24-ounce) bag frozen large cheese ravioli
- ☐ 1 (16-ounce) bag frozen mixed berries
- ☐ 1 (16-ounce) bag frozen peeled and deveined large shrimp
- ☐ 1 (28-ounce) bag frozen hash brown potatoes

Dairy/Eggs
- ☐ 1 pint half-and-half
- ☐ 1 pint buttermilk
- ☐ 1 pint heavy whipping cream
- ☐ 1 (8-ounce) package cream cheese
- ☐ 1 (8-ounce) bag shredded Cheddar cheese

- ☐ 1 (8-ounce) bag shredded mozzarella cheese
- ☐ 1 (5.3-ounce) container plain 2% Greek yogurt
- ☐ 1 (8-ounce) container whole milk ricotta cheese
- ☐ 1 pound salted butter
- ☐ 1 pound unsalted butter
- ☐ 1 dozen large eggs

Bulk Foods
- ☐ ½ cup granola cereal
- ☐ ¼ cup sliced almonds

Canned and Jarred Foods
- ☐ 1 (6-ounce) jar pitted black olives
- ☐ 1 (4-ounce) tube tomato paste
- ☐ 1 (15-ounce) can chickpeas
- ☐ 1 (4-ounce) jar diced pimentos
- ☐ 1 (4-ounce) jar Thai red curry paste
- ☐ 1 (8-ounce) jar dill pickle relish
- ☐ 1 (5-ounce) bottle hot sauce
- ☐ 1 (15-ounce) can crushed tomatoes
- ☐ 1 (32-ounce) container low-sodium vegetable broth

- ☐ 1 (32-ounce) container low-sodium beef broth
- ☐ 1 (6.5-ounce) jar basil pesto
- ☐ 1 (10-ounce) jar apricot jam
- ☐ 1 (12-ounce) jar honey
- ☐ 1 (12.5-ounce) bottle red wine vinegar
- ☐ 1 (7.5-ounce) jar Dijon mustard
- ☐ 1 (15-ounce) can full-fat coconut milk
- ☐ 1 (15.5-ounce) jar marinara sauce
- ☐ 1 (8-ounce) jar mayonnaise
- ☐ 1 (5-ounce) bottle Worcestershire sauce
- ☐ 1 (8-ounce) bottle yellow mustard

Dry Goods
- ☐ 1 (16-ounce) box dried rotini pasta
- ☐ 1 (16-ounce) box dried fettuccine pasta
- ☐ 1 (16-ounce) bag medium-grain white rice
- ☐ 1 (8-ounce) box panko bread crumbs

Alcohol
- ☐ 1 (750ml) bottle dry white wine
- ☐ 1 (750ml) bottle bourbon
- ☐ 1 (750ml) bottle brandy

WEEK 1: *Prep List*

Sunday
- Prepare two servings of Pimento Cheese Spread.
- Prepare Honey Mustard–Roasted Chicken Legs through Step 1 and refrigerate.
- Prepare Traditional Potato Salad and refrigerate.

- Prepare Italian Rotini Salad and refrigerate.
- Prepare Freeze and Bake Chocolate Chip Cookies and freeze.
- Freeze remaining whole-grain bread; reserve one slice for Thursday's breakfast.

WEEK 2: MEAL PLAN

	Breakfast	Lunch	Snack	Dinner	Dessert
Sunday	Ham and Cheddar Frittata	Asparagus Risotto	Creamy Ranch Deviled Eggs*	Pasta Bolognese*	Fresh Peach Cupcakes**
Monday	Make-Ahead Ham, Egg, and Cheese Sandwiches*	Chopped House Salad with Ranch	Almond and Cheddar–Stuffed Dates	Braised Beef Short Rib Potatoes au Gratin	Fresh Peach Cupcakes**
Tuesday	Peanut Butter Banana Smoothie	Mediterranean Pasta Salad*	Creamy Ranch Deviled Eggs**	Creamy Pesto Ravioli	Banana Pudding for One
Wednesday	Apple and Brown Sugar Breakfast Cookies*	Pasta Bolognese**	Almond and Date Energy Bites	Parchment-Baked Salmon Buttery Herb Rice	No-Bake Cheesecake with Berry Sauce
Thursday	Make-Ahead Ham, Egg, and Cheese Sandwiches**	Mediterranean Pasta Salad**	Sweet and Salty Granola Bars*	Spinach and Feta–Stuffed Mushroom or Dine Out	Freeze and Bake Chocolate Chip Cookies**
Friday	Apple and Brown Sugar Breakfast Cookies**	Chopped House Salad with Ranch or Dine Out	Fresh Tomato Salsa	Barbecue-Glazed Meatloaf Twice-Baked Potato with Broccoli*	Freeze and Bake Chocolate Chip Cookies**
Saturday	Hearty Vegetable Scramble	Baked Cheeseburger Sliders	Sweet and Salty Granola Bars**	Vegetable Lover's Pizza	Crème Brûlée

*Prep-Ahead Recipe
**Planned Leftovers

WEEK 2: *Shopping List*

Deli
- [ ] ¼ pound sliced American cheese
- [ ] 4 ounces crumbled feta cheese
- [ ] 2 ounces sliced Cheddar cheese

Bakery
- [ ] 1 (4-count) package Hawaiian rolls
- [ ] 1 (6-count) package white English muffins
- [ ] 1 (10-ounce) package ready-to-bake 8" pizza crusts

Meat and Seafood
- [ ] 1 (8-ounce) bone-in English beef short rib
- [ ] 16 ounces 90/10 ground beef
- [ ] 4 ounces ground pork
- [ ] 1 (4-ounce) salmon filet
- [ ] 1 (12-ounce) package bacon

Produce
- [ ] 3 large bananas
- [ ] 1 head broccoli
- [ ] 1 (8-ounce) container whole button mushrooms
- [ ] 1 medium carrot
- [ ] 1 bunch celery
- [ ] 1 English cucumber
- [ ] 2 Granny Smith apples
- [ ] 1 head iceberg lettuce
- [ ] 2 large portobello mushroom caps
- [ ] 1 medium red bell pepper
- [ ] 1 head romaine lettuce
- [ ] 1 (8-ounce) russet potato

- [ ] 1 (6-ounce) Yukon Gold potato
- [ ] 3 small yellow onions
- [ ] 1 small red onion
- [ ] 1 medium lemon
- [ ] 1 medium lime
- [ ] 1 medium Roma tomato
- [ ] 1 jalapeño
- [ ] 1 (0.5-ounce) pack fresh dill
- [ ] 1 (10-ounce) bag fresh baby spinach
- [ ] 1 bunch fresh parsley

Baking Needs
- [ ] 1 (12-ounce) jar molasses
- [ ] 1 (16-ounce) bottle corn syrup
- [ ] 1 (12-ounce) bag mini semisweet chocolate chips

Dairy/Eggs
- [ ] 1 (8-ounce) package cream cheese
- [ ] 1 (8-ounce) bag shredded Cheddar cheese
- [ ] 2 dozen large eggs
- [ ] 1 quart whole milk
- [ ] 1 (8-ounce) container plain 2% Greek yogurt
- [ ] 1 (8-ounce) container sour cream

Bulk Foods
- [ ] 2 cups pitted Medjool dates
- [ ] ⅓ cup Arborio rice
- [ ] ¼ cup dried cherries
- [ ] 1 cup roasted, unsalted whole pecans
- [ ] 4 cups roasted, unsalted whole almonds

☐ ¼ cup unsweetened coconut flakes
☐ ½ cup quick-cooking oats

Canned and Jarred Foods
☐ 1 (15-ounce) can crushed tomatoes
☐ 1 (12-ounce) jar almond butter
☐ 1 (12-ounce) jar creamy peanut butter
☐ 1 (4.6-ounce) jar kalamata olives
☐ 1 (6.5-ounce) jar marinated
  artichoke hearts
☐ 1 (14-ounce) bottle ketchup

Dry Goods
☐ 1 (16-ounce) box dried penne pasta
☐ 1 (16-ounce) box dried orzo pasta
☐ 1 (18-ounce) container rolled oats
☐ 1 (11-ounce) box vanilla wafer cookies

Alcohol
☐ 1 (750ml) bottle dry red wine

WEEK 2: *Prep List*

Sunday

- Prepare 2 servings ranch dressing as instructed in Step 1 of Chopped House Salad with Ranch.
- Prepare Almond and Cheddar–Stuffed Dates through step 2, cover, and refrigerate.
- Prepare Make-Ahead Ham, Egg, and Cheese Sandwiches.

- Chop vegetables for Mediterranean Pasta Salad.
- Prepare Potatoes au Gratin through Step 2, cover, and refrigerate.
- Freeze remaining English muffins.

WEEK 3: MEAL PLAN

	Breakfast	Lunch	Snack	Dinner	Dessert
Sunday	Apple and Brown Sugar Breakfast Cookies**	Pork Egg Roll in a Bowl	Spiced Baked Tortilla Chips	Portobello Mushroom Parmesan Seven Layer Salad	Spiced Bread and Butter Pudding
Monday	Sausage, Egg, and Cheese Breakfast Burrito	Chicken and Green Chili Stacked Enchiladas	Sweet and Salty Granola Bars**	Peach-Glazed Pork Chop* Twice-Baked Potato with Broccoli**	Freeze and Bake Chocolate Chip Cookies**
Tuesday	Honey Ricotta Toast with Fresh Strawberries	Soba Noodles with Peanut Sauce or Dine Out	Honey-Roasted Almonds*	Pan-Fried Trout with Lemon Butter Roasted Asparagus with Lemon and Parmesan	Fresh Peach Cupcakes**
Wednesday	Peach, Granola, and Yogurt Breakfast Parfait	Black Bean Tacos with Corn and Tomato Relish	Sweet and Salty Granola Bars**	Chicken Fajitas Vegetarian Charro Beans*	Freeze and Bake Chocolate Chip Cookies**
Thursday	Easy Migas	Peach-Glazed Pork Chop** Buttery Herb Rice	Honey-Roasted Almonds**	Ground Beef Chili*	Fresh Peach Cupcakes**
Friday	Chia Pudding with Almond Butter and Berries*	Cacio e Pepe	Egg Salad for One	Orzo and Vegetable–Stuffed Pepper or Dine Out	Molten Chocolate Cake
Saturday	Blueberry Buttermilk Muffins*	Spinach and Cheddar Twice-Baked Potato	Fresh Tomato Salsa	Ground Beef Chili**	Rustic Apple Cinnamon Tart

*Prep-Ahead Recipe

**Planned Leftovers

Deli
- [ ] 16 ounces shredded rotisserie chicken breast

Bakery
- [ ] 1 (16-ounce) package 24-count 6" corn tortillas
- [ ] 1 small loaf white sandwich bread
- [ ] 1 loaf brioche bread
- [ ] 1 (16-ounce) package 8" flour tortillas

Meat and Seafood
- [ ] 8 ounces 90/10 ground beef
- [ ] 1 (6-ounce) boneless, skinless chicken breast
- [ ] 2 (6-ounce) boneless pork chops
- [ ] 1 (6-ounce) rainbow trout filet
- [ ] 8 ounces smoked sausage

Produce
- [ ] 1 bunch fresh cilantro
- [ ] 1 (14-ounce) bag coleslaw mix
- [ ] 1 bunch green onions
- [ ] 2 medium lemons
- [ ] 1 medium peach
- [ ] 2 medium red bell peppers
- [ ] 3 medium Roma tomatoes
- [ ] 1 (8-ounce) russet potato
- [ ] 1 (8-ounce) bag fresh baby spinach
- [ ] 1 medium orange
- [ ] 1 (16-ounce) container fresh strawberries
- [ ] 1 (6-ounce) package fresh blueberries
- [ ] 1 bunch asparagus
- [ ] 1 small red onion
- [ ] 1 medium lime
- [ ] 1 jalapeño pepper
- [ ] 2 medium yellow onions

Baking Needs
- [ ] 1 (4-ounce) jar vanilla bean paste

Freezer
- [ ] 1 (10-ounce) bag frozen corn
- [ ] 1 (10-ounce) bag frozen peas
- [ ] 1 (16-ounce) bag frozen blueberries

Dairy/Eggs
- [ ] 1 pint heavy whipping cream
- [ ] 1 pint buttermilk
- [ ] 1 dozen large eggs
- [ ] 1 (5.3-ounce) container plain 2% Greek yogurt
- [ ] 1 (8-ounce) bag shredded sharp Cheddar cheese
- [ ] 1 (8-ounce) bag shredded mozzarella cheese
- [ ] 1 (8-ounce) container sour cream
- [ ] 1 (8-ounce) container whole milk ricotta cheese
- [ ] 1 pound salted butter
- [ ] 1 pound unsalted butter

Bulk Foods
- [ ] ¼ cup chia seeds

Canned and Jarred Foods
- ☐ 1 (15-ounce) can black beans
- ☐ 1 (15-ounce) can pinto beans
- ☐ 1 (9-ounce) bottle oyster sauce
- ☐ 1 (8.5-ounce) jar hoisin sauce
- ☐ 1 (10-ounce) bottle light soy sauce
- ☐ 1 (10-ounce) bottle rice wine vinegar
- ☐ 1 (7.41-ounce) jar chili crisp, such as Laoganma
- ☐ 1 (8-ounce) bottle toasted sesame oil
- ☐ 1 (10-ounce) can green chili enchilada sauce
- ☐ 1 (7-ounce) can chipotle peppers in adobo
- ☐ 1 (16-ounce) jar tomato salsa
- ☐ 1 (10-ounce) jar sweet pickle relish
- ☐ 1 (32-ounce) container low-sodium vegetable broth
- ☐ 1 (32-ounce) container low-sodium beef broth

Dry Goods
- ☐ 1 (16-ounce) box dried spaghetti pasta
- ☐ 1 (9.5-ounce) packet dried soba noodles

WEEK 3: *Prep List*

Sunday

- Prepare Chicken and Green Chili Stacked Enchiladas through Step 3, cover, and refrigerate.
- Set aside ½ cup shredded rotisserie chicken breast (place in an airtight container in the refrigerator) for Chicken and Green Chili Stacked Enchiladas. Freeze remaining shredded rotisserie chicken breast.
- Prepare peanut sauce for Soba Noodles with Peanut Sauce and refrigerate (Step 1 of recipe).
- Prepare relish for Black Bean Tacos with Corn and Tomato Relish and refrigerate (Step 1 of recipe).
- Set aside 1 (¼"-thick) slice brioche bread for Tuesday's Honey Ricotta Toast with Fresh Strawberries.
- Freeze remaining brioche bread.

Monday

- Thaw 2 Fresh Peach Cupcakes overnight in an airtight container in the refrigerator.

WEEK 4: MEAL PLAN

	Breakfast	Lunch	Snack	Dinner	Dessert
Sunday	Chia Pudding with Almond Butter and Berries**	Vegetable and Lentil Stew*	Pimento Cheese Spread	Shrimp and Grits	Chocolate Cupcakes* (freeze 4 cupcakes)
Monday	Blueberry Buttermilk Muffins**	Spinach and Cheddar Twice-Baked Potato	Peanut Butter Cream Cheese Dip	Stacked Black Bean and Cheese Enchiladas Vegetarian Charro Beans**	Chocolate Cupcakes** (freeze 5 cupcakes)
Tuesday	Loaded Avocado Toast with Smoked Salmon	Baked Rotini with Ricotta	Creamy Ranch Deviled Eggs*	Egg Noodle Stir-Fry	Lemon Blueberry Pound Cake*
Wednesday	Ham and Cheddar Breakfast Bake*	Vegetable and Lentil Stew**	Toasted Baguette with Brie and Jam	Miso-Glazed Salmon Saffron Rice	Freeze and Bake Chocolate Chip Cookies**
Thursday	Loaded Avocado Toast with Smoked Salmon	Quick Black Bean Soup	Creamy Ranch Deviled Eggs**	Garlic Butter Shrimp Pasta or Dine Out	Lemon Blueberry Pound Cake**
Friday	Ham and Cheddar Breakfast Bake**	Soba Noodles with Peanut Sauce	Toasted Baguette with Brie and Jam	Chicken Tetrazzini	Carrot Cake*
Saturday	Fluffy Buttermilk Pancakes with Bourbon Maple Syrup	Creamy Mushroom Soup or Dine Out	Pizza Rolls	Seasoned Steamed Crab Legs Buttery Herb Rice	Cheesecake for One

Prep-Ahead Recipe
**Planned Leftovers*

Deli
- ☐ 1 (6-ounce) wedge Brie cheese
- ☐ 8 ounces Canadian bacon
- ☐ 1 (6-ounce) package sliced pepperoni

Bakery
- ☐ 1 demi-baguette

Meat and Seafood
- ☐ 1 (8-ounce) package smoked salmon
- ☐ ½ pound raw snow crab legs
- ☐ 1 (4-ounce) salmon filet

Produce
- ☐ 1 large avocado
- ☐ 1 (8-ounce) container sliced button mushrooms
- ☐ 1 large carrot
- ☐ 1 (16-ounce) bag coleslaw mix
- ☐ 1 bunch celery
- ☐ 1 bulb garlic
- ☐ 2 medium lemons
- ☐ 1 (8-ounce) russet potato
- ☐ 1 (5-ounce) russet potato
- ☐ 1 bunch green onions
- ☐ 1 medium Roma tomato
- ☐ 1 bunch fresh parsley

Baking Needs
- ☐ 1 (2.2-ounce) jar toasted sesame seeds
- ☐ 1 (2-ounce) jar Old Bay seasoning

Freezer
- ☐ 1 (16-ounce) bag frozen stir-fry vegetables
- ☐ 1 (20-ounce) bag frozen root vegetables

Dairy/Eggs
- ☐ 1 pint half-and-half
- ☐ 1 pint whole milk
- ☐ 1 (9-ounce) jar clarified butter
- ☐ 1 (8-ounce) package cream cheese
- ☐ 2 dozen large eggs
- ☐ 1 (8-ounce) bag shredded mozzarella cheese
- ☐ 1 (8-ounce) bag shredded sharp Cheddar cheese

Bulk Foods
- ☐ ½ cup dried green lentils
- ☐ ¼ cup walnuts

Canned and Jarred Foods
- ☐ 1 (15-ounce) can black beans
- ☐ 1 (13-ounce) jar fig jam
- ☐ 1 (10-ounce) can green enchilada sauce
- ☐ 1 (32-ounce) container low-sodium chicken broth

Dry Goods
- ☐ 1 (16-ounce) box dried linguini pasta
- ☐ 1 (16-ounce) box uncooked corn grits
- ☐ 1 (16-ounce) bag dried lo mein noodles
- ☐ 1 (14.4-ounce) box graham crackers

WEEK 4: *Prep List*

Sunday

- Prepare Pimento Cheese Spread.
- Prepare peanut sauce for Soba Noodles with Peanut Sauce and refrigerate (Step 1 of recipe).
- Prepare Spinach and Cheddar Twice-Baked Potato through Step 7, cover, and refrigerate.
- Prepare Ham and Cheddar Breakfast Bake through Step 3 and refrigerate.

Monday

- Thaw 2 slices whole-grain bread overnight in an airtight container in the refrigerator.

Thursday

- Thaw ½ cup shredded rotisserie chicken breast for Chicken Tetrazzini overnight in an airtight container in the refrigerator.

WEEK 5: MEAL PLAN

	Breakfast	Lunch	Snack	Dinner	Dessert
Sunday	Ham and Cheddar Breakfast Bake*	Baked Rotini with Ricotta	Cranberry Brie Mini Tarts	Gnocchi with Creamy Mushroom Sauce	Carrot Cake**
Monday	Peach Mango Smoothie	Seven Layer Salad or Dine Out	Almond and Cheddar–Stuffed Dates	Cranberry Turkey Meatballs* Honey-Glazed Carrots	Chocolate Cupcakes**
Tuesday	Sausage, Egg, and Cheese Breakfast Burrito	Chicken Noodle Soup	Pimento Cheese Spread	Summer Vegetable Flatbread	Pecan Blondies* (freeze 2 blondies)
Wednesday	Ham and Cheddar Breakfast Bake**	Mushroom Gyro	Cranberry Brie Mini Tarts	Garlic Scampi Buttery Herb Rice	Pecan Blondies**
Thursday	Peach Mango Smoothie	Cranberry Turkey Meatballs** Buttery Herb Rice	Almond and Cheddar–Stuffed Dates	Cauliflower Fried Rice or Dine Out	Banana Pudding for One
Friday	Easy Migas	Vegetable Summer Rolls	Spiced Baked Tortilla Chips	Sweet and Sour Pork	Pecan Blondies**
Saturday	Almond Butter Baked Oatmeal	Spinach and Feta–Stuffed Mushroom	Everything Pigs in a Blanket	Cassoulet with White Beans*	Pecan Blondies**

*Prep-Ahead Recipe
**Planned Leftovers

WEEK 5: *Shopping List*

Deli
- [ ] 4 ounces crumbled feta cheese

Bakery
- [ ] 1 (11-ounce) package pita bread

Meat and Seafood
- [ ] 6 ounces pork butt
- [ ] 8 ounces ground turkey breast
- [ ] 1 (4-ounce) boneless, skinless chicken breast

Produce
- [ ] 1 (16-ounce) bottle orange juice
- [ ] 1 (8-ounce) bag baby carrots
- [ ] 1 medium banana
- [ ] 1 (8-ounce) container sliced button mushrooms
- [ ] 1 (8-ounce) container cherry tomatoes
- [ ] 1 English cucumber
- [ ] 1 head iceberg lettuce
- [ ] 2 large portobello mushroom caps
- [ ] 1 small red onion
- [ ] 1 small white onion
- [ ] 1 medium red bell pepper
- [ ] 1 (8-ounce) bag fresh baby spinach
- [ ] 1 small head purple cabbage
- [ ] 3 small yellow onions
- [ ] 1 medium zucchini
- [ ] 1 large avocado
- [ ] 1 bunch fresh cilantro
- [ ] 1 medium lemon

- [ ] 1 medium lime
- [ ] 4 medium Roma tomatoes
- [ ] 1 (0.5-ounce) container fresh mint
- [ ] 1 (0.5-ounce) container fresh basil
- [ ] 1 (0.5-ounce) container fresh rosemary

Baking Needs
- [ ] 1 (1.75-ounce) jar Chinese five-spice powder
- [ ] 1 (1.5-ounce) poultry seasoning

Freezer
- [ ] 1 (16-ounce) bag frozen mango chunks
- [ ] 1 (16-ounce) bag frozen peach slices
- [ ] 1 (1.9-ounce) package baked phyllo tart shells
- [ ] 1 (10-ounce) bag frozen riced cauliflower

Dairy/Eggs
- [ ] 1 pint buttermilk
- [ ] 1 (8-ounce) bag shredded sharp Cheddar cheese
- [ ] 1 (8-ounce) container plain 2% Greek yogurt
- [ ] 1 pint half-and-half
- [ ] 1 (8-ounce) container whole milk ricotta cheese
- [ ] 1 (8-ounce) container sour cream
- [ ] 1 pound salted butter
- [ ] 1 pound unsalted butter
- [ ] 1 dozen large eggs

Bulk Foods

☐ 1 cup roasted, unsalted whole pecans

Canned and Jarred Foods

☐ 1 (15-ounce) can whole-berry cranberry sauce

☐ 1 (15-ounce) can cannellini beans

☐ 1 (15-ounce) can crushed tomatoes

☐ 1 (8-ounce) can pineapple juice

Dry Goods

☐ 1 (16-ounce) package dried potato gnocchi

☐ 1 (4-ounce) package rice paper wrappers

☐ 1 (8.8-ounce) box thin rice noodles

☐ 1 (15-ounce) box bread crumbs

Alcohol

☐ 1 (750ml) bottle dry white wine

WEEK 5: *Prep List*

Sunday

- Prepare Pimento Cheese Spread.
- Prepare Almond and Cheddar–Stuffed Dates through Step 2, cover, and refrigerate.
- Prepare Chicken Noodle Soup, cover, and refrigerate.
- Prepare dressing for Seven Layer Salad (Step 1 of recipe) and refrigerate.
- Thaw 1 Chocolate Cupcake overnight in an airtight container in the refrigerator.

Saturday

- Thaw 1 Pecan Blondie overnight in an airtight container in the refrigerator for next Sunday's snack.

WEEK 6: MEAL PLAN

	Breakfast	Lunch	Snack	Dinner	Dessert
Sunday	Ham and Sweet Potato Hash	Italian Rotini Salad*	Pecan Blondies**	Creamy Seafood Chowder*	Freeze and Bake Oatmeal Cookies*
Monday	Make-Ahead Ham, Egg, and Cheese Sandwiches*	Cassoulet with White Beans**	Everything Pigs in a Blanket	Egg Noodle Stir-Fry	Chocolate Cupcakes**
Tuesday	Chia Pudding with Almond Butter and Berries*	Italian Rotini Salad**	Pecan Blondies**	Herbed Couscous–Stuffed Zucchini	Lemon Blueberry Pound Cake*
Wednesday	Make-Ahead Ham, Egg, and Cheese Sandwiches**	Creamy Seafood Chowder**	Honey-Roasted Almonds*	Mussels in Spicy Tomato Sauce	Freeze and Bake Oatmeal Cookies**
Thursday	Peanut Butter Banana Smoothie	Sesame Garlic Soba Noodles or Dine Out	Creamy Fruit Dip*	Baked Crab Cake with Rémoulade	Lemon Blueberry Pound Cake**
Friday	Chia Pudding with Almond Butter and Berries**	Mediterranean Pasta Salad*	Honey-Roasted Almonds**	Miso-Glazed Salmon or Dine Out	No-Bake Cheesecake with Berry Sauce
Saturday	Ham and Cheddar Scones*	Mushroom Gyro	Toasted Ravioli	Baked Macaroni and Cheese for One	Freeze and Bake Oatmeal Cookies**

Prep-Ahead Recipe
**Planned Leftovers*

WEEK 6: *Shopping List*

Deli
- [ ] 8 ounces Canadian bacon
- [ ] 2 ounces sliced Cheddar cheese

Meat and Seafood
- [ ] 1 (8-ounce) can lump crab meat
- [ ] 1 (4-ounce) salmon filet
- [ ] 1 (8-ounce) cod filet
- [ ] 8 ounces smoked sausage

Produce
- [ ] 1 large banana
- [ ] 1 (6-ounce) container fresh blueberries
- [ ] 1 (16-ounce) container fresh strawberries
- [ ] 1 bunch green onions
- [ ] 1 medium lemon
- [ ] 2 large portobello mushroom caps
- [ ] 1 medium sweet potato
- [ ] 1 medium zucchini
- [ ] 1 English cucumber
- [ ] 1 medium red onion
- [ ] 1 bunch fresh parsley
- [ ] 1 (8-ounce) container cherry tomatoes
- [ ] 1 bunch celery
- [ ] 1 medium carrot
- [ ] 1 small Yukon Gold potato
- [ ] 1 medium yellow onion
- [ ] 1 large red bell pepper
- [ ] 1 medium Roma tomato

Baking Needs
- [ ] 1 (2.25-ounce) jar Cajun seasoning

Freezer
- [ ] 1 (16-ounce) bag frozen stir-fry vegetables
- [ ] 1 (16-ounce) bag frozen peeled and deveined large shrimp
- [ ] 1 (8-ounce) bag frozen cleaned mussels

Dairy/Eggs
- [ ] 1 dozen large eggs
- [ ] 1 pint heavy whipping cream
- [ ] 1 pint buttermilk
- [ ] 1 (8-ounce) bag shredded mozzarella cheese
- [ ] 1 (8-ounce) package cream cheese
- [ ] 1 pint whole milk
- [ ] 1 (8-ounce) bag shredded sharp Cheddar cheese
- [ ] 1 (5.3-ounce) container plain 2% Greek Yogurt

Bulk Foods
- [ ] ¼ cup chia seeds
- [ ] ¼ cup couscous

Canned and Jarred Foods
- [ ] 1 (15-ounce) can crushed tomatoes
- [ ] 1 (4-ounce) jar diced pimentos
- [ ] 1 (8-ounce) jar whole-grain mustard

☐ 1 (32-ounce) container low-sodium vegetable broth

☐ 1 (14.5-ounce) can seafood stock

☐ 1 (17-ounce) bottle hot chili sauce, such as Sriracha

☐ 1 (15.5-ounce) jar marinara sauce

Dry Goods

☐ 1 (16-ounce) box dried rotini pasta

☐ 1 (16-ounce) box dried macaroni pasta

WEEK 6: *Prep List*

Sunday

- Chop vegetables for Mediterranean Pasta Salad.
- Prepare Make-Ahead Ham, Egg, and Cheese Sandwiches.
- Thaw 2 English muffins overnight in an airtight container in the refrigerator.

Monday

- Thaw 1 Chocolate Cupcake overnight in an airtight container in the refrigerator.
- Thaw 1 Pecan Blondie overnight in an airtight container in the refrigerator.

WEEK 7: MEAL PLAN

	Breakfast	Lunch	Snack	Dinner	Dessert
Sunday	Ham and Cheddar Frittata	Chicken and Green Chili Stacked Enchiladas	Creamy Fruit Dip**	Chicken Potpie	Freeze and Bake Snickerdoodles*
Monday	Ham and Cheddar Scones**	Mediterranean Pasta Salad**	Chunky Guacamole	Herb-Crusted Steelhead Trout Roasted Asparagus with Lemon and Parmesan	Mixed-Berry Crumble
Tuesday	Hearty Vegetable Scramble	Chicken Noodle Soup	Sweet and Salty Granola Bars*	Panang Curry with Chicken	Chocolate Cupcakes**
Wednesday	Peach, Granola, and Yogurt Breakfast Parfait	Soba Noodles with Peanut Sauce	Chunky Guacamole	Asparagus Risotto	Freeze and Bake Snickerdoodles**
Thursday	Blueberry Buttermilk Muffins*	Chickpea Masala* Saffron Rice	Chunky Guacamole	Cajun Chicken Pasta or Dine Out	Chocolate Cupcakes**
Friday	Blueberry Buttermilk Muffins**	Spinach and Cheddar Twice-Baked Potato	Sweet and Salty Granola Bars**	Pasta Primavera	Chocolate Chip Brownies* (freeze 1 brownie)
Saturday	Almond Butter Baked Oatmeal	Chickpea Masala* Saffron Rice or Dine Out	Everything Pigs in a Blanket	Beef Short Rib Pot Roast* Whipped Yukon Gold Potato with Chives	Chocolate Chip Brownies**

*Prep-Ahead Recipe

**Planned Leftovers

Meat and Seafood

- [ ] 3 (4-ounce) boneless, skinless chicken breasts
- [ ] 1 (4-ounce) steelhead trout filet
- [ ] 16 ounces bone-in English beef short ribs, bones removed

Produce

- [ ] 1 bunch asparagus
- [ ] 1 large avocado
- [ ] 1 head broccoli
- [ ] 1 medium green bell pepper
- [ ] 1 medium lemon
- [ ] 1 medium peach
- [ ] 1 large red bell pepper
- [ ] 2 medium Roma tomatoes
- [ ] 1 (8-ounce) russet potato
- [ ] 1 (8-ounce) bag fresh baby spinach
- [ ] 1 small yellow onion
- [ ] 1 medium yellow squash
- [ ] 1 (6-ounce) Yukon Gold potato
- [ ] 1 medium zucchini
- [ ] 1 cup baby potatoes
- [ ] 1 (16-ounce) bag coleslaw mix
- [ ] 1 bunch fresh cilantro
- [ ] 1 (8-ounce) container whole button mushrooms
- [ ] 1 (0.5-ounce) container fresh basil
- [ ] 1 medium lime

Baking Needs

- [ ] 1 (1.5-ounce) jar cream of tartar
- [ ] 1 (2-ounce) jar instant espresso powder

Freezer

- [ ] 1 (12-ounce) bag frozen mixed vegetables

Dairy/Eggs

- [ ] 1 pint whole milk
- [ ] 1 (8-ounce) container sour cream
- [ ] 1 pint buttermilk
- [ ] 1 dozen large eggs
- [ ] 1 (5.3-ounce) container plain 2% Greek yogurt
- [ ] 1 (8-ounce) shredded sharp Cheddar cheese

Bulk Foods

- [ ] ⅓ cup Arborio rice
- [ ] ¼ cup dried cherries

Canned and Jarred Foods

- [ ] 1 (15-ounce) can chickpeas
- [ ] 1 (32-ounce) container low-sodium beef broth
- [ ] 1 (15-ounce) can full-fat coconut milk
- [ ] 1 (16-ounce) jar panang curry paste
- [ ] 1 (10-ounce) can green chili enchilada sauce
- [ ] 1 (15-ounce) can black beans

Dry Goods

- [ ] 1 (16-ounce) packet dried soba noodles

Alcohol

- [ ] 1 (750ml) bottle dry red wine
- [ ] 1 (750ml) bottle dry white wine

Sunday

- Prepare peanut sauce for Soba Noodles with Peanut Sauce and refrigerate (Step 1 of recipe).
- Thaw 2 cups shredded rotisserie chicken breast.

Monday

- Thaw 2 Chocolate Cupcakes overnight in an airtight container in the refrigerator.

Saturday

- Thaw 1 slice of whole-grain bread overnight in an airtight container in the refrigerator for next Sunday's breakfast.

WEEK 8: MEAL PLAN

	Breakfast	Lunch	Snack	Dinner	Dessert
Sunday	Loaded Avocado Toast with Smoked Salmon	Baked California Roll Casserole	Pizza Rolls	Lobster Macaroni and Cheese	Chocolate Chip Brownies**
Monday	Peanut Butter Banana Smoothie	Spaghetti with Tangy Tomato Sauce	Sweet and Salty Granola Bars**	Beef Short Rib Pot Roast** Potatoes au Gratin	Freeze and Bake Snickerdoodles**
Tuesday	Loaded Avocado Toast with Smoked Salmon	Garlic Butter Shrimp Pasta or Dine Out	Egg Salad for One	Seared Beef Filet with Herb Butter Twice-Baked Potato with Broccoli*	Chocolate Chip Brownies**
Wednesday	Easy Migas	Creamy Mushroom Soup	Sweet and Salty Granola Bars*	Crispy Fried Shrimp Chopped House Salad with Ranch	Freeze and Bake Oatmeal Cookies**
Thursday	Peanut Butter Banana Smoothie	Baked Rotini with Ricotta	Fresh Tomato Salsa	Gnocchi with Brown Butter and Sage or Dine Out	Freeze and Bake Snickerdoodles**
Friday	Honey Ricotta Toast with Fresh Strawberries	Panang Curry with Chicken	Peanut Butter Cream Cheese Dip	Beef and Pork Meatballs* Whipped Yukon Gold Potato with Chives	Chocolate Chip Brownies**
Saturday	Fluffy Buttermilk Pancakes with Bourbon Maple Syrup	Beef and Pork Meatballs** Macaroni Salad	Everything Pigs in a Blanket	Lobster Thermidor Twice-Baked Potato with Broccoli**	Molten Chocolate Cake

*Prep-Ahead Recipe
**Planned Leftovers

Deli
☐ 1 (4-ounce) package smoked salmon

Bakery
☐ 1 (16-ounce) package 24-count 6"
    corn tortillas

Meat and Seafood
☐ 6 ounces 90/10 ground beef
☐ 1 (8-ounce) filet mignon
☐ 1 (3-ounce) package imitation crab
☐ 1 (8-ounce) raw lobster tail
☐ 1 (3-ounce) package ready-to-eat
    lobster meat
☐ 1 (4-ounce) boneless, skinless
    chicken breast
☐ 8 ounces smoked sausage
☐ 6 ounces ground pork

Produce
☐ 1 large avocado
☐ 2 large bananas
☐ 1 (8-ounce) container sliced button
    mushrooms
☐ 1 bunch celery
☐ 1 (8-ounce) container cherry
    tomatoes
☐ 1 bunch fresh cilantro
☐ 1 English cucumber
☐ 1 head iceberg lettuce
☐ 1 small red onion
☐ 1 head romaine lettuce
☐ 1 (8-ounce) russet potato
☐ 1 small yellow onion

☐ 1 medium orange
☐ 1 medium lime
☐ 1 medium lemon
☐ 1 jalapeño pepper
☐ 1 large red bell pepper
☐ 2 (6-ounce) Yukon Gold potatoes
☐ 1 (0.5-ounce) container fresh basil
☐ 1 bunch fresh parsley
☐ 2 medium Roma tomatoes
☐ 1 (16-ounce) container fresh
    strawberries

Freezer
☐ 1 (16-ounce) bag frozen peeled and
    deveined large shrimp

Dairy/Eggs
☐ 1 dozen large eggs
☐ 1 (8-ounce) container 2%
    plain Greek yogurt
☐ 1 (8-ounce) package cream cheese
☐ 1 pint heavy whipping cream
☐ 1 pint whole milk
☐ 1 (8-ounce) container whole milk
    ricotta cheese
☐ 1 (8-ounce) bag shredded Gruyère
    cheese
☐ 1 (8-ounce) bag shredded sharp
    Cheddar cheese
☐ 1 (8-ounce) bag shredded mozzarella
    cheese

Bulk Foods
☐ 1 cup pitted Medjool dates

Canned and Jarred Foods

☐ 1 (15-ounce) can crushed tomatoes

☐ 1 (10-ounce) bottle sushi vinegar

☐ 1 (1.5-ounce) tube prepared wasabi

☐ 1 (12-ounce) bottle Japanese-style mayonnaise, such as Kewpie

☐ 1 (32-ounce) container low-sodium vegetable broth

☐ 1 (15.5-ounce) jar marinara sauce

Dry Goods

☐ 1 (1-ounce) package nori sheets

☐ 1 (1.7-ounce) jar furikake

☐ 1 (17.8-ounce) box Ritz crackers

☐ 1 (7-ounce) package cooked short-grain rice

WEEK 8: *Prep List*

Sunday

- Prepare Potatoes au Gratin through Step 2, cover, and refrigerate.

Monday

- Thaw 1 slice of whole-grain bread overnight in an airtight container in the refrigerator.

Thursday

- Thaw 1 slice of brioche bread overnight in an airtight container in the refrigerator.
- Thaw 1 Chocolate Chip Brownie overnight in an airtight container in the refrigerator.

BREAKFAST

The morning can be hectic when you are getting ready for a busy day, but planning your weekly breakfasts ahead of time makes things much easier. From recipes ready in 10 minutes or less to make-ahead meals you can easily reheat and eat on your way out the door, meal planning for one ensures you can enjoy a delicious breakfast in less time, with less stress, and with less waste!

This chapter has recipes that provide variety and flexibility and that can blend seamlessly into a weekly meal plan. Get a healthy start to your day with Loaded Avocado Toast with Smoked Salmon or a cool Peach Mango Smoothie, each ready in less than 10 minutes. When you know you will be on the go, you can plan in advance and have Make-Ahead Ham, Egg, and Cheese Sandwiches and Blueberry Buttermilk Muffins ready to go. For mornings when you can cook (and eat) at your leisure, try the Almond Butter Baked Oatmeal or Ham and Sweet Potato Hash. These recipes will ensure you have a tasty breakfast for one to start the day right!

PEACH, GRANOLA, AND YOGURT BREAKFAST PARFAIT

PREP TIME: 10 MINUTES | COOK TIME: 3 MINUTES | SERVES 1

This fruity and refreshing parfait is a delicious way to start your day. The other half of the peach used in this recipe can be used to make the Peach-Glazed Pork Chop (Chapter 9) or Fresh Peach Cupcakes (Chapter 10). Be sure to add the granola just before serving to keep it crisp!

INGREDIENTS

1 tablespoon sliced almonds

½ fresh medium peach, pitted and diced

2 teaspoons honey, divided

⅛ teaspoon ground cinnamon

1 (5.3-ounce) container plain 2% Greek yogurt

¼ teaspoon pure vanilla extract

2 tablespoons granola

1. In an 8" nonstick skillet over medium heat, add almonds. Cook, stirring constantly, until lightly toasted, about 3 minutes. Set aside and cool to room temperature, about 10 minutes.

2. To a small bowl, add peach, 1 teaspoon honey, and cinnamon and toss well to coat. Set aside.

3. In a separate small bowl, add remaining 1 teaspoon honey, yogurt, and vanilla. Mix well to combine.

4. To a serving bowl or parfait dish, add ⅓ of yogurt mixture, ½ of peach mixture, and ½ of toasted almonds. Repeat layering, ending with a layer of yogurt. Cover and refrigerate 1 hour, up to 3 days. Top with granola before serving.

PER SERVING

Calories: 271
Fat: 7g
Protein: 18g
Sodium: 55mg

Fiber: 3g
Carbohydrates: 36g
Sugar: 27g

HAM AND CHEDDAR BREAKFAST BAKE

PREP TIME: 10 MINUTES | COOK TIME: 40 MINUTES | SERVES 2

 Planning for leftovers is a great strategy to save time on busy days. This savory bake makes two servings, and the extra portion can be refrigerated for up to 5 days. When you're ready to eat, just reheat it in a 350°F oven for 10 minutes, in the air fryer at 350°F for 8 minutes, or in the microwave on high for 45–50 seconds until hot.

INGREDIENTS

3 large eggs, beaten

3 tablespoons half-and-half

1 teaspoon freeze-dried chives

⅛ teaspoon hot sauce

⅛ teaspoon salt

⅛ teaspoon freshly cracked black pepper

⅓ cup frozen hash brown potatoes

¼ cup cubed Canadian bacon

2 tablespoons diced yellow onion

½ cup shredded medium Cheddar cheese

1. Preheat oven to 375°F and spray a 1-quart baking dish with nonstick cooking spray.

2. In a medium bowl, combine eggs, half-and-half, chives, hot sauce, salt, and pepper. Set aside.

3. In prepared casserole dish, layer potatoes, Canadian bacon, onion, and Cheddar. Pour egg mixture over top.

4. Bake 35–40 minutes or until casserole is golden brown and puffed all over and a paring knife inserted into center comes out clean. Cool 5 minutes before slicing and serving.

PER SERVING

Calories: 330   Fiber: 1g
Fat: 18g   Carbohydrates: 10g
Protein: 26g   Sugar: 2g
Sodium: 790mg

FLUFFY BUTTERMILK PANCAKES WITH BOURBON MAPLE SYRUP

PREP TIME: 10 MINUTES | COOK TIME: 10 MINUTES | SERVES 1

 Buttermilk helps these pancakes stay light and fluffy while adding a bit of tangy zip to the flavor. Buttermilk is also used in the recipe for Chocolate Cupcakes (Chapter 10), which could make a great dessert addition to your weekly meal plan!

INGREDIENTS

3 tablespoons maple syrup

1 teaspoon bourbon

½ cup all-purpose flour

1 teaspoon baking powder

¼ teaspoon baking soda

¹⁄₁₆ teaspoon sea salt

1 large egg, beaten

¼ cup buttermilk

2 teaspoons unsalted butter, melted

1 teaspoon granulated sugar

¼ teaspoon pure vanilla extract

1. In a 1-quart saucepan, add maple syrup. Heat over medium-low heat until mixture starts to simmer, about 2 minutes. Remove from heat and immediately stir in bourbon. Set aside.

2. Preheat a nonstick skillet or griddle over medium-low heat. If using griddle, lightly coat griddle with nonstick cooking spray.

3. In a medium bowl, sift together flour, baking powder, baking soda, and salt, then whisk well to combine. Make a well in the center of flour mixture and add egg, buttermilk, butter, sugar, and vanilla to well. Mix until just combined and only small lumps remain, about ten strokes. Let stand 3 minutes.

4. Pour ½ of batter onto the prepared griddle or skillet. Cook 2 minutes or until top of pancake is bubbling and edges look dry, flip, and cook 1–2 minutes more until the center of the pancake springs back when gently pressed. Transfer to a plate and repeat with remaining batter.

5. Serve pancakes immediately with bourbon maple syrup over top.

PER SERVING

Calories: 477	Fiber: 1g
Fat: 14g	Carbohydrates: 69g
Protein: 15g	Sugar: 20g
Sodium: 671mg	

HAM AND CHEDDAR SCONES

PREP TIME: 10 MINUTES | COOK TIME: 18 MINUTES | YIELDS 4 SCONES

The recipe for this elegant, savory scone is portioned to make two servings of two scones each. Leftover scones should be eaten within 3 days and should be stored in the refrigerator in an airtight container. To reheat, just bake at 350°F for 10 minutes or microwave on high for 10–12 seconds until warm.

INGREDIENTS

½ cup plus 2 tablespoons all-purpose flour, plus extra for dusting

½ teaspoon baking powder

½ teaspoon granulated sugar

⅛ teaspoon dried mustard powder

2 tablespoons salted butter, cubed and chilled

⅓ cup shredded Cheddar cheese

¼ cup chopped Canadian bacon

¼ cup heavy whipping cream

1 large egg yolk

1. Preheat oven to 350°F and line a ¼ sheet pan with baking parchment or a silicone baking mat.

2. In a small bowl, combine flour, baking powder, sugar, and mustard powder. Add butter and, with your fingers, rub until the butter is in pea-sized pieces and the flour resembles sand. Toss in Cheddar and Canadian bacon and mix well. Cover and refrigerate 10 minutes.

3. Make a well in flour mixture and add cream and egg yolk to well. Gently whisk egg yolk with cream, then stir in flour mixture until it just forms a shaggy ball. Turn out onto a lightly floured surface and press dough into a ½"-thick rectangle, then fold dough in half. Use a spatula or bench scraper if needed for the first few times to assist, as dough will be shaggy. Turn dough a quarter turn and repeat this process four more times. Cover dough and refrigerate 10 minutes.

4. Use your hands to form chilled dough into a ¾"-thick circle. Use a sharp chef's knife and cut the circle into four wedges by pressing straight down and lifting straight up. Transfer wedges to prepared sheet pan.

5. Bake 15–18 minutes until scones are puffed and golden brown. Cool on the pan 5 minutes before enjoying.

PER SERVING (2 SCONES)

Calories: 500	*Fiber: 1g*
Fat: 30g	*Carbohydrates: 33g*
Protein: 20g	*Sugar: 3g*
Sodium: 680mg	

HEARTY VEGETABLE SCRAMBLE

PREP TIME: 10 MINUTES | COOK TIME: 8 MINUTES | SERVES 1

 Vegetable lovers will adore this scramble packed with bell pepper, mushrooms, and broccoli and topped with melted Cheddar cheese. You can use fresh or frozen vegetables here or change the variety of vegetables, so if you have some vegetables left from the prior week's meal plan, you can use them here.

INGREDIENTS

2 teaspoons olive oil, divided

¼ cup chopped yellow onion

¼ cup finely chopped broccoli florets

¼ cup chopped red bell pepper

3 large button mushrooms, trimmed and chopped

⅛ teaspoon sea salt

2 large eggs

1 teaspoon freeze-dried chives

¼ teaspoon freshly cracked black pepper

2 tablespoons shredded Cheddar cheese

1. Heat an 8" nonstick skillet over medium heat. Add 1 teaspoon oil and swirl to coat pan. Add onion, broccoli, bell pepper, mushrooms, and salt. Sauté until vegetables are soft, about 5 minutes. Transfer cooked vegetables to a medium bowl and set aside.

2. Wipe out pan and return to heat. Add remaining 1 teaspoon oil and swirl to coat pan. Beat eggs with chives and black pepper until fluffy and well combined. Add eggs to pan and reduce heat to low. Let pan stand 20 seconds or until eggs start to set, then use a silicone or other heatproof spatula to gently push edges of eggs to center of pan while tilting so uncooked eggs move to edges, about 30 seconds.

3. Once eggs are just starting to form curds, add cooked vegetables. Continue to cook, gently pulling eggs from edges of pan to the center until cooked to your preference, about 1 minute for soft-set eggs and 2 minutes for firm-set eggs.

4. Transfer to a serving plate and sprinkle Cheddar over top. Serve immediately.

PER SERVING

Calories: 329   Fiber: 3g

Fat: 22g   Carbohydrates: 11g

Protein: 20g   Sugar: 5g

Sodium: 439mg

LOADED AVOCADO TOAST WITH SMOKED SALMON

PREP TIME: 5 MINUTES | COOK TIME: 0 MINUTES | SERVES 1

 Smoked salmon is a beloved accompaniment to creamy avocado, and it keeps fresh for up to 1 week when stored in an airtight container in the refrigerator. When adding this recipe to your weekly meal plan, consider including the Creamy Smoked Salmon Pasta (Chapter 6) later in the week for lunch or dinner.

INGREDIENTS

1 slice whole-grain bread, toasted

⅓ cup mashed avocado

¼ teaspoon fresh lemon juice

2 ounces sliced smoked salmon

1 large hard-boiled egg, sliced

1 tablespoon finely minced red onion

1 tablespoon finely minced English cucumber

¼ teaspoon everything bagel seasoning

On toasted bread, spread avocado in an even layer. Sprinkle lemon juice over avocado. Top with smoked salmon and egg, then sprinkle onion, cucumber, and everything bagel seasoning over top. Serve immediately.

Keeping Cut Avocado Fresh
Depending on your meal plan, you may have fresh avocado left over after you have made a recipe. If you are planning to use your avocado within 24 hours, simply put it in the refrigerator uncovered. If you are going to use it later in the week, spritz it with lemon juice and wrap it tightly in plastic wrap before refrigerating.

PER SERVING

Calories: 355	Fiber: 8g
Fat: 18g	Carbohydrates: 21g
Protein: 22g	Sugar: 3g
Sodium: 635mg	

EASY MIGAS

PREP TIME: 10 MINUTES | COOK TIME: 5 MINUTES | SERVES 1

 This warm and filling recipe is a great place to use leftover corn tortillas and Cheddar cheese from the Stacked Black Bean and Cheese Enchiladas (Chapter 7) or Chicken and Green Chili Stacked Enchiladas (Chapter 9). Consider including this recipe during weeks when you add those recipes to your weekly meal plan!

INGREDIENTS

2 tablespoons vegetable oil

2 (6") yellow corn tortillas, cut into 6 wedges

2 large eggs

⅛ teaspoon sea salt

⅛ teaspoon ground cumin

¼ cup tomato salsa

¼ cup shredded Cheddar cheese

2 tablespoons finely chopped red onion

1 tablespoon finely chopped fresh cilantro

1. Heat an 8" nonstick skillet over medium heat. Add oil and swirl to coat pan. Add tortilla wedges and cook, flipping often, until crisp, about 2 minutes. Transfer to a paper towel–lined plate and set aside.

2. Wipe out pan and return to heat. Beat eggs in a small bowl with salt and cumin until fluffy and well combined. Add eggs to pan and reduce heat to low. Let pan stand 20 seconds or until eggs start to set, then add salsa and fried tortillas. Start gently pulling eggs from edges of pan and folding over fried tortillas until everything is well mixed and cooked to your preference, about 1 minute for soft-set eggs and 2 minutes for firm-set eggs.

3. Transfer to a serving plate and sprinkle Cheddar, onion, and cilantro over top. Serve immediately.

Storing Fresh Herbs

For storing tender herbs such as cilantro and parsley, trim the ends, then place the herbs in a jar filled with ½" of water, cover loosely with a plastic bag, and refrigerate. Basil should be trimmed and stored in a jar of water but left out at room temperature. Hardy herbs like rosemary and thyme should be wrapped in a damp paper towel and stored in a bag in the refrigerator.

PER SERVING

Calories: 443   Fiber: 4g

Fat: 30g   Carbohydrates: 24g

Protein: 16g   Sugar: 2g

Sodium: 370mg

HONEY RICOTTA TOAST WITH FRESH STRAWBERRIES

PREP TIME: 10 MINUTES | COOK TIME: 6 MINUTES | SERVES 1

 Ricotta will stay fresh in the refrigerator for up to 2 weeks, so you can include it in 2 weeks of meal plans. This rich and sweet recipe is a must for meal plans that also include Ravioli Lasagna (Chapter 6) or Summer Vegetable Flatbread (Chapter 7).

INGREDIENTS

3 tablespoons whole milk ricotta cheese

1 tablespoon honey, divided

¼ teaspoon pure vanilla extract

¼ teaspoon fresh orange zest

1 (½"-thick) slice brioche bread

1 teaspoon unsalted butter, melted

¼ cup sliced fresh strawberries

⅛ teaspoon ground cinnamon

1. In a small bowl, add ricotta, 2 teaspoons honey, vanilla, and orange zest. Using a small whisk, whip ricotta until light and fluffy, about 2 minutes. Set aside or cover and refrigerate overnight.

2. Heat an 8" skillet over medium heat. Brush both sides of bread with butter. Grill bread for 2–3 minutes per side until toasted and lightly brown.

3. Transfer to a serving plate. Spread whipped ricotta over toast. Top with strawberry slices, and drizzle with remaining 1 teaspoon honey. Sprinkle with cinnamon. Serve immediately.

Seasonal Eating

One way to save money on your food budget while meal planning is to shop your produce seasonally. For example, in this recipe, you can swap the strawberries, at their freshest in spring, for thin wedges of peach in summer, diced apple in the fall, and pomegranate arils in winter.

PER SERVING

Calories: 300
Fat: 11g
Protein: 9g
Sodium: 229mg
Fiber: 1g
Carbohydrates: 43g
Sugar: 22g

PEANUT BUTTER BANANA SMOOTHIE

PREP TIME: 5 MINUTES | COOK TIME: 0 MINUTES | SERVES 1

 This smoothie is creamy, filling, and packed with protein and fiber. It's the perfect breakfast for busy mornings and should be considered for meal plans that include Barbecue-Glazed Meatloaf (Chapter 9), which includes both oats and date too!

INGREDIENTS

½ cup whole milk

½ cup plain 2% Greek yogurt

1 large banana, peeled, cut into 1" chunks, and frozen

3 tablespoons rolled oats

2 tablespoons creamy peanut butter

2 pitted Medjool dates

⅛ teaspoon ground cinnamon

Add all ingredients to a blender. Purée until smooth, about 1 minute. Serve immediately.

PER SERVING

Calories: 567   Fiber: 8g
Fat: 23g   Carbohydrates: 70g
Protein: 26g   Sugar: 40g
Sodium: 95mg

PEACH MANGO SMOOTHIE

PREP TIME: 5 MINUTES | COOK TIME: 0 MINUTES | SERVES 1

 Frozen fruit chunks are ideal staple items to have on hand when you meal plan for one. They keep fresh for up to 3 months for cold, creamy, and utterly delicious smoothies. Frozen fruit chunks are also a yummy snack on a hot day!

INGREDIENTS

½ cup orange juice

½ cup plain 2% Greek yogurt

½ cup frozen mango chunks

½ cup frozen peach slices

1 tablespoon honey

Add all ingredients to a blender. Purée until smooth, about 1 minute. Serve immediately.

Make It a Smoothie Bowl

You can transform most smoothies into smoothie bowls by adding toppings used in other meal prep during the week. For example, add some granola used in the Peach, Granola, and Yogurt Breakfast Parfait along with some berries and chia seeds from the Chia Pudding with Almond Butter and Berries.

PER SERVING

Calories: 288   Fiber: 3g

Fat: 3g   Carbohydrates: 56g

Protein: 14g   Sugar: 50g

Sodium: 39mg

CHIA PUDDING WITH ALMOND BUTTER AND BERRIES

PREP TIME: 10 MINUTES | COOK TIME: 0 MINUTES | SERVES 2

 Chia seed puddings can be made ahead and refrigerated for up to 5 days to enjoy on busy mornings. If you prefer a creamier texture, purée the milk, chia seeds, almond butter, maple syrup, vanilla, and cinnamon in a blender for 1 minute. This also helps make them easier to digest.

INGREDIENTS

1 cup whole milk

¼ cup chia seeds

3 tablespoons almond butter

2 tablespoons maple syrup

¼ teaspoon pure vanilla extract

¼ teaspoon ground cinnamon

½ cup fresh blueberries

½ cup diced fresh strawberries

1. In a medium bowl, add milk, chia seeds, almond butter, maple syrup, vanilla, and cinnamon and mix well. Let stand 5 minutes, then mix again. Cover and refrigerate overnight.

2. To serve, scoop ½ of pudding mixture into a serving bowl. Top with ¼ cup each blueberries and strawberries. Serve immediately.

PER SERVING

Calories: 446   Fiber: 14g

Fat: 24g   Carbohydrates: 45g

Protein: 14g   Sugar: 25g

Sodium: 60mg

ALMOND BUTTER BAKED OATMEAL

PREP TIME: 10 MINUTES | COOK TIME: 35 MINUTES | SERVES 1

 To make your morning easier, you can mix up this filling oatmeal the evening before, transfer it to the dish, cover, and refrigerate, then pop it in a preheated oven the next morning. This recipe uses a lot of kitchen staples such as oats, eggs, and milk, so it makes an easy addition to your weekly meal plan!

INGREDIENTS

½ cup whole milk

1 large egg, beaten

2 tablespoons packed light brown sugar

2 tablespoons almond butter

1 tablespoon unsalted butter, melted

¼ teaspoon pure vanilla extract

½ cup rolled oats

¼ teaspoon baking powder

⅛ teaspoon salt

1. Preheat oven to 350°F and spray a ½-quart baking dish with nonstick cooking spray.

2. In a small bowl, add milk and egg. Mix well, then add sugar, almond butter, butter, and vanilla and mix until smooth. Add oats, baking powder, and salt and mix to combine.

3. Transfer oatmeal mixture to prepared dish. Bake 30–35 minutes until oatmeal is set and golden brown on top. Cool 5 minutes before serving.

Reheating Baked Oatmeal

Baked oatmeal can be made up to 3 days in advance and reheated before serving if you prefer to make it ahead of time for a busy morning. To reheat, either warm covered with aluminum foil in a 350°F oven for 15 minutes or microwave on high for 1–2 minutes until steaming hot.

PER SERVING

Calories: 699   Fiber: 7g
Fat: 38g   Carbohydrates: 67g
Protein: 22g   Sugar: 36g
Sodium: 544mg

MAKE-AHEAD HAM, EGG, AND CHEESE SANDWICHES

PREP TIME: 5 MINUTES | COOK TIME: 5 MINUTES | SERVES 2

 These classic sandwiches can be made with any fully cooked breakfast meat you prefer, so if you have bacon or breakfast sausage on hand, you can use that here. The sandwiches stay fresh for up to 4 days in the refrigerator or can be wrapped in aluminum foil and frozen for up to 3 months—just thaw overnight and heat as directed.

INGREDIENTS

2 slices Canadian bacon

2 large eggs, lightly beaten

2 teaspoons heavy whipping cream

½ teaspoon freeze-dried chives

⅛ teaspoon freshly cracked black pepper

⅛ teaspoon sea salt

1 teaspoon vegetable oil

2 white English muffins, sliced in half

2 slices Cheddar cheese

1. In an 8" skillet over medium heat, add Canadian bacon. Cook until lightly brown on both sides, about 45 seconds per side. Transfer to a plate and set aside.

2. In a medium bowl, whisk together eggs, cream, chives, pepper, and salt.

3. Add oil to the same skillet and swirl pan to coat. Add egg mixture to pan and let stand 30 seconds, then reduce heat to low. Let eggs cook until just set, about 1½ minutes, then carefully flip and let cook 30–45 seconds or until egg is cooked through.

4. Remove egg to a cutting board and cut in half, then fold each half in half to form two triangles.

5. Place 1 slice Canadian bacon on bottom of 1 English muffin, add egg, then top with 1 slice Cheddar. Add top of muffin. Repeat to make second sandwich. Wrap each sandwich in baking parchment, then place into a resealable bag and refrigerate for up to 4 days.

6. To serve, heat sandwich wrapped in paper in the microwave on high 1 minute, then flip and heat 20–30 seconds more until steamy hot. Let stand 1 minute before unwrapping and enjoying.

PER SERVING

Calories: 377　Fiber: 2g
Fat: 18g　Carbohydrates: 26g
Protein: 23g　Sugar: 3g
Sodium: 767mg

APPLE AND BROWN SUGAR BREAKFAST COOKIES

PREP TIME: 10 MINUTES | COOK TIME: 16 MINUTES | YIELDS 6 COOKIES

 This recipe makes six chewy, hearty, fruit-and-oat packed breakfast cookies that yield three servings of two cookies each. Extra cookies keep for up to 4 days in an airtight container at room temperature or can be frozen for up to 3 months and thawed overnight in the refrigerator before eating. No need to wait until after dinner to enjoy a delectable cookie or two!

INGREDIENTS

½ cup creamy peanut butter

1 medium banana, peeled and mashed

3 tablespoons packed light brown sugar

½ teaspoon pure vanilla extract

¼ teaspoon sea salt

½ teaspoon ground cinnamon

1 cup quick-cooking oats

½ cup chopped Granny Smith apple

¼ cup chopped roasted, unsalted pecans

3 pitted Medjool dates, chopped

1. Preheat oven to 325°F and line a ¼ sheet pan with baking parchment.

2. In a medium bowl, use a hand mixer on medium speed to combine peanut butter, banana, and sugar, about 30 seconds. Add vanilla, salt, and cinnamon and mix until well combined, about 30 seconds.

3. With a spatula, fold in oats, apple, pecans, and dates until evenly combined.

4. Scoop dough into six mounds and place on prepared sheet pan 2" apart. Bake 14–16 minutes until cookies are brown and soft but not gooey. Cool completely on pan, about 30 minutes.

Breakfast Cookie Variations

To change these cookies up, you can make any of the following swaps: ripe pear for apple, almond butter for peanut butter, raisins or dried cranberries for dates, chocolate chips or your favorite chopped nuts for pecans, or cardamom for cinnamon.

PER SERVING (2 COOKIES)

Calories: 542   Fiber: 8g

Fat: 29g   Carbohydrates: 60g

Protein: 15g   Sugar: 30g

Sodium: 142mg

HAM AND SWEET POTATO HASH

PREP TIME: 10 MINUTES | COOK TIME: 34 MINUTES | SERVES 1

 Sweet potatoes give this hash a sweet, earthy flavor that pairs well with salty Canadian bacon. Canadian bacon is also used in the Make-Ahead Ham, Egg, and Cheese Sandwiches in this chapter as well as in the Quick Black Bean Soup (Chapter 5).

INGREDIENTS

1 tablespoon vegetable oil

¾ cup diced sweet potato

¼ cup diced yellow onion

¼ cup diced red bell pepper

1 clove garlic, peeled and minced

¼ teaspoon sea salt

¼ teaspoon freshly cracked black pepper

¼ teaspoon ground cumin

¼ teaspoon smoked paprika

¼ cup chopped Canadian bacon

1 large egg

1. Preheat oven to 400°F.

2. Heat an 8" ovenproof skillet over medium heat. Once hot, add oil and swirl to coat skillet. Add sweet potato and cook, stirring often, 10 minutes. Add onion and bell pepper and continue to cook, stirring often, until sweet potato is fork-tender, 5–10 minutes.

3. Add garlic, salt, black pepper, cumin, and paprika to skillet and stir to combine. Add Canadian bacon and cook 2 minutes, then create a well in center of skillet and add egg to well.

4. Place skillet in oven and bake 10–12 minutes until egg is set but yolk is still soft. Cool 2 minutes before serving.

PER SERVING

Calories: 384   Fiber: 5g
Fat: 20g   Carbohydrates: 29g
Protein: 22g   Sugar: 8g
Sodium: 991mg

BLUEBERRY BUTTERMILK MUFFINS

PREP TIME: 10 MINUTES | COOK TIME: 20 MINUTES | YIELDS 4 MUFFINS

 This bake once, eat twice recipe makes four sweet and fluffy muffins, two muffins per serving. Extra muffins keep beautifully for up to 3 days in an airtight container at room temperature or can be frozen for up to 1 month. Frozen muffins just need to thaw overnight in the refrigerator before they're ready to be enjoyed.

INGREDIENTS

½ cup all-purpose flour, divided

¼ cup frozen blueberries

¼ cup granulated sugar

¼ teaspoon baking powder

⅛ teaspoon ground cinnamon

⅛ teaspoon baking soda

⅛ teaspoon salt

¼ cup buttermilk

1 large egg, at room temperature

1 tablespoon unsalted butter, melted and cooled

¼ teaspoon pure vanilla extract

1. Preheat oven to 350°F and line four cups of a six-cup muffin pan with paper liners.

2. In a small bowl, add 1 teaspoon flour and blueberries. Gently toss until berries are coated in flour. Set aside.

3. In a medium bowl, add remaining flour, sugar, baking powder, cinnamon, baking soda, and salt. Whisk to combine. Set aside.

4. In another small bowl, whisk together buttermilk, egg, butter, and vanilla. Pour wet ingredients into dry ingredients and use a spatula to mix until just combined, about six strokes, then add blueberries and fold to combine, 4–6 strokes. Do not overmix.

5. Divide batter among prepared muffin cups. Bake 18–20 minutes until muffins spring back when gently pressed in the center and tops are golden brown. Let cool in pan 3 minutes, then transfer to a wire rack to cool to room temperature, about 30 minutes.

PER SERVING (2 MUFFINS)

Calories: 325   Fiber: 1g
Fat: 9g   Carbohydrates: 53g
Protein: 8g   Sugar: 28g
Sodium: 352mg

SAUSAGE, EGG, AND CHEESE BREAKFAST BURRITO

PREP TIME: 5 MINUTES | COOK TIME: 5 MINUTES | SERVES 1

 Burritos make a terrific warm, handheld breakfast on the go. You can make this burrito the evening before, wrap it in parchment, and refrigerate. The next morning, just heat it up for 1 minute on high in the microwave, flip to the other side, and heat 20 seconds more. Let stand 1 minute before eating.

INGREDIENTS

2 ounces diced smoked sausage

2 tablespoons diced red bell pepper

2 tablespoons diced yellow onion

1 large egg, beaten

⅛ teaspoon sea salt

⅛ teaspoon freshly cracked black pepper

1 (8") flour tortilla

1 tablespoon tomato salsa

2 tablespoons shredded Cheddar cheese

1. Heat an 8" nonstick skillet over medium heat. Add sausage and cook 30 seconds, then add bell pepper and onion. Sauté until vegetables are soft, about 3 minutes.

2. Lower heat to low and add egg, salt, and black pepper. Cook, stirring often, until egg is cooked thoroughly, about 1 minute.

3. Place tortilla on a heat-safe plate and microwave on high 15 seconds to soften, then add cooked egg mixture to the center. Top with salsa and Cheddar. Pull top of tortilla over eggs, tuck sides of tortilla into center, then roll forward to form a burrito. Enjoy immediately.

Make It a Quesadilla

Transform your breakfast burrito into a toasty quesadilla! Once the fillings are cooked, transfer them to a bowl and wipe out the pan. Place a tortilla in the pan and scoop fillings over half of the tortilla. Top with salsa and Cheddar, then fold the tortilla over the fillings. Cook over medium heat until golden brown on both sides, about 2 minutes per side.

PER SERVING

Calories: 458   Fiber: 3g

Fat: 25g   Carbohydrates: 31g

Protein: 21g   Sugar: 4g

Sodium: 1,298mg

HAM AND CHEDDAR FRITTATA

PREP TIME: 5 MINUTES | COOK TIME: 13 MINUTES | SERVES 1

 This simple frittata is a wonderful addition to an egg lover's meal plan. It's also a good place to use up extra eggs and Canadian bacon left over from other recipes you've cooked that week. Pair this with toast or a bowl of fruit for an elegant morning treat. This also makes a nice dinner paired with Roasted Broccoli (Chapter 5).

INGREDIENTS

1 teaspoon salted butter

2 tablespoons diced yellow onion

¼ cup diced Canadian bacon

⅓ cup shredded Cheddar cheese, divided

½ teaspoon freeze-dried chives

¼ teaspoon freshly cracked black pepper

⅛ teaspoon flaky sea salt

⅛ teaspoon ground nutmeg

2 large eggs, beaten

1. Preheat broiler to 550°F.

2. In an 8" oven-safe skillet over medium heat, add butter. Once melted and foaming, about 20 seconds, swirl to coat pan, then add onion. Cook until onion starts to soften, about 1 minute. Add Canadian bacon and cook until it is hot and starting to brown slightly, about 2 minutes.

3. Sprinkle bacon mixture with ¼ cup Cheddar, chives, pepper, salt, and nutmeg. Pour eggs evenly over top. Reduce heat to medium-low and cook 3–4 minutes until bottom of eggs are just set. Top with remaining Cheddar.

4. Transfer pan to oven and broil 3–5 minutes until top of frittata is set and lightly browned. Remove from oven and cool 3 minutes before serving.

PER SERVING

Calories: 410   Fiber: 1g

Fat: 25g   Carbohydrates: 4g

Protein: 35g   Sugar: 2g

Sodium: 1,093mg

CHAPTER 4

SNACKS AND TREATS

Snacks are an important part of your weekly meal plan as they help curb your appetite between meals, give you a boost of energy when you hit the late-afternoon slump, and help you savor those more relaxed moments. While you can buy ready-made snacks at the store, there is something satisfying about making custom snacks in portions for one that slip easily into a weekly meal plan. Snacks on a weekly meal plan are also helpful for reducing waste and carryover from week to week.

In this chapter, you will find sweet treats and savory snacks that you can easily plug into your own weekly meal plan. For a busy day when you need an energy boost on the go, why not try Almond and Date Energy Bites or Sweet and Salty Granola Bars? Looking for an indulgent snack? Toasted Ravioli or Everything Pigs in a Blanket fit the bill. And if an elegant snack is what you want, look no further than Toasted Baguette with Brie and Jam or Cranberry Brie Mini Tarts. These recipes will keep you satisfied all day long!

CHUNKY GUACAMOLE

PREP TIME: 5 MINUTES | COOK TIME: 0 MINUTES | SERVES 1

 Enjoy this easy guacamole as a snack with tortilla chips, or serve it along with the Sausage, Egg, and Cheese Breakfast Burrito (Chapter 3); Black Bean Tacos with Corn and Tomato Relish (Chapter 7); or Chicken and Green Chili Stacked Enchiladas (Chapter 9).

INGREDIENTS

½ large avocado, pitted, peeled, and diced, divided

2 tablespoons diced Roma tomato

1 tablespoon diced yellow onion

1 teaspoon chopped fresh cilantro

½ teaspoon fresh lime juice

⅛ teaspoon ground cumin

⅛ teaspoon sea salt

In a small bowl, add ½ of avocado chunks. Mash with a fork until smooth. Add remaining avocado chunks along with remaining ingredients and fold to combine. Cover and refrigerate 20 minutes before serving.

Make Guacamole Ahead

To keep guacamole fresh for up to 3 days, prepare as directed in the recipe. Scoop into an airtight container and spread smooth. Spritz the top with juice from one lime wedge, about ½ teaspoon, then place a layer of plastic wrap directly on guacamole. Cover container and refrigerate until ready to enjoy.

PER SERVING

Calories: 122   Fiber: 5g

Fat: 9g   Carbohydrates: 8g

Protein: 2g   Sugar: 1g

Sodium: 201mg

TOASTED RAVIOLI

PREP TIME: 10 MINUTES | COOK TIME: 3 MINUTES | SERVES 1

 Toasted Ravioli are a great treat for when you want to indulge. If you are a sports fan, add these to your meal plan for game day to enjoy while you watch your big game! Add this snack to your meal plan when you are also making Ravioli Lasagna or Creamy Pesto Ravioli (both in Chapter 6) to use up the remaining ravioli.

INGREDIENTS

1 large egg, beaten

¼ cup panko bread crumbs

¼ teaspoon Italian seasoning

5 large frozen cheese ravioli

Vegetable oil, for frying

2 teaspoons grated Parmesan cheese

¼ cup marinara sauce

1. In a shallow dish, add egg. To a separate shallow dish, add bread crumbs and Italian seasoning and mix well.

2. Dip frozen ravioli, one at a time, into beaten egg, then roll in bread crumb mixture. Place on a small tray and return to freezer while you heat oil.

3. In a medium pot with deep sides, add enough oil to fill to 1" deep. Heat over medium heat until oil reaches 350°F. Add ravioli to pot and fry until golden brown on each side, about 1 minute per side.

4. Transfer fried ravioli to a paper towel–lined tray and sprinkle with Parmesan. Let rest 1 minute (ravioli will continue to cook as they rest).

5. While ravioli rest, heat marinara in microwave on high 30 seconds or until warm. Serve ravioli with marinara on the side for dipping.

PER SERVING

Calories: 648   Fiber: 3g

Fat: 32g   Carbohydrates: 69g

Protein: 19g   Sugar: 7g

Sodium: 751mg

PIMENTO CHEESE SPREAD

PREP TIME: 5 MINUTES | COOK TIME: 0 MINUTES | SERVES 1

 This spicy cheese spread is delicious with crackers or spread into celery sticks, but you can also use it on sandwiches, so it is a versatile and tasty addition to your weekly meal plan!

INGREDIENTS

¼ cup shredded sharp Cheddar cheese

1 tablespoon drained and dried diced pimentos

1 tablespoon mayonnaise

2 teaspoons cream cheese, at room temperature

⅛ teaspoon hot sauce

⅛ teaspoon Worcestershire sauce

⅛ teaspoon smoked paprika

Combine all ingredients in a small bowl. Cover and refrigerate at least 1 hour before serving, up to 3 days. Enjoy chilled or at room temperature.

Grilled Pimento Cheese Sandwich

Turn this spread into the perfect filling of a grilled cheese sandwich! Spread the prepared pimento cheese between two ¼"-thick slices sourdough bread. Butter the outside of each slice with ½ teaspoon salted butter. Heat a small skillet over medium heat. Grill the sandwich 3–4 minutes per side until golden brown and crisp. Let the sandwich rest 1 minute before enjoying.

PER SERVING

Calories: 308   Fiber: 0g
Fat: 27g   Carbohydrates: 3g
Protein: 9g   Sugar: 2g
Sodium: 400mg

CREAMY FRUIT DIP

PREP TIME: 5 MINUTES | COOK TIME: 0 MINUTES | SERVES 2

 This combination of cream and fruit is a scrumptious way to use extra cream cheese from meal plans that also include Pimento Cheese Spread (in this chapter), Baked California Roll Casserole (Chapter 8), or No-Bake Cheesecake with Berry Sauce (Chapter 10).

INGREDIENTS

2 ounces cream cheese, at room temperature

2 tablespoons heavy whipping cream, cold

2 tablespoons confectioners' sugar

¼ teaspoon pure vanilla extract

¼ teaspoon ground cinnamon

1 cup fresh strawberries, divided

1. In a small bowl, add cream cheese and heavy whipping cream. With a spatula, beat mixture until well combined, about 1 minute. Add sugar, vanilla, and cinnamon and beat 1–2 minutes more until mixture is fluffy and well combined.

2. Cover bowl and refrigerate at least 1 hour, up to 3 days, before serving with ½ cup strawberries.

PER SERVING

Calories: 227   Fiber: 3g
Fat: 14g   Carbohydrates: 21g
Protein: 3g   Sugar: 16g
Sodium: 109mg

EGG SALAD FOR ONE

PREP TIME: 10 MINUTES | COOK TIME: 0 MINUTES | SERVES 1

 Want to use eggs in your meal plan outside of breakfast? Look no further! Enjoy as is, or use this egg salad to top crackers or toasted bread. If you do not have relish on hand, feel free to mince any pickles you have, or omit.

INGREDIENTS

2 large hard-boiled eggs, finely chopped

1 tablespoon mayonnaise

1 teaspoon minced yellow onion

1 teaspoon sweet pickle relish

½ teaspoon yellow mustard

¼ teaspoon freeze-dried dill

⅛ teaspoon sea salt

⅛ teaspoon freshly cracked black pepper

⅛ teaspoon sweet paprika

1. Combine eggs and mayonnaise in a medium bowl. Add onion, relish, mustard, dill, salt, and pepper and mix well to combine.

2. Transfer mixture to serving bowl and garnish with paprika. Cover and refrigerate at least 1 hour, up to 4 days. Serve chilled.

Hard-Boiled Eggs

To hard-boil the perfect egg, add to a pot and cover with cold water. Place over medium-high heat and bring to a rolling boil, then turn off the heat, cover pot with a lid, and let stand 12 minutes. Rinse under cool water, peel, and refrigerate for up to 7 days.

PER SERVING

Calories: 254
Fat: 19g
Protein: 13g
Sodium: 488mg
Fiber: 0g
Carbohydrates: 3g
Sugar: 1g

SWEET AND SALTY GRANOLA BARS

PREP TIME: 10 MINUTES | COOK TIME: 8 MINUTES | YIELDS 4 BARS

 Granola bars make a tasty snack or treat on the go, can be added to a simple breakfast of yogurt or fruit to add extra nutrition, and keep for up to 2 weeks in the refrigerator. Just one batch can work for four meals and snacks over 2 weeks of meals plans!

INGREDIENTS

1 cup rolled oats

¼ cup chopped roasted, unsalted pecans

2 tablespoons unsalted butter

2 tablespoons packed light brown sugar

2 tablespoons creamy peanut butter

1 tablespoon corn syrup

¼ teaspoon pure vanilla extract

¼ cup chopped dried cherries

¼ teaspoon sea salt, divided

1. Preheat oven to 350°F and line a ¼ sheet pan with baking parchment.

2. Spread oats and pecans on prepared sheet pan. Bake 4–5 minutes, stirring every minute, until oats and pecans are well toasted. Set aside to cool, about 10 minutes.

3. In a small saucepan, add butter, sugar, peanut butter, and corn syrup. Stir well, then heat over medium heat until sugar is melted and edges start to bubble, about 3 minutes.

4. Transfer butter mixture to a medium bowl and add oats, pecans, and vanilla. Mix until well combined, then fold in dried cherries and ⅛ teaspoon salt.

5. Lightly spray a 4" square baking dish with nonstick cooking spray, then add a strip of baking parchment that hangs over pan by 4" and spray with nonstick cooking spray. Press granola mixture firmly into pan, then sprinkle top with remaining ⅛ teaspoon salt.

6. Refrigerate 2 hours, then lift by parchment, remove from dish, and cut into four bars. Store in an airtight container in the refrigerator. Enjoy chilled or at room temperature.

PER SERVING (1 BAR)

Calories: 296   Fiber: 3g
Fat: 15g   Carbohydrates: 35g
Protein: 5g   Sugar: 19g
Sodium: 105mg

FRESH TOMATO SALSA

PREP TIME: 10 MINUTES | COOK TIME: 0 MINUTES | SERVES 1

 Salsa tastes best if allowed to sit for a couple of hours so the flavors can mingle, so allow for this time when making the following recipe. Enjoy this salsa with the Spiced Baked Tortilla Chips in this chapter for a tasty, healthy treat to add to your meal plan!

INGREDIENTS

1 medium Roma tomato, seeded and chopped

2 tablespoons chopped yellow onion

1 tablespoon chopped fresh cilantro

1 teaspoon minced jalapeño

2 teaspoons fresh lime juice

¼ teaspoon ground cumin

⅛ teaspoon sea salt

Combine all ingredients in a small bowl. Cover and refrigerate at least 2 hours, up to 3 days. Serve chilled or at room temperature.

Make It Fruity

Have peach on your meal plan for making Fresh Peach Cupcakes (Chapter 10)? Dice up 3 tablespoons of peach flesh and add to this salsa. It will transform the flavor with a subtle sweet kick!

PER SERVING

Calories: 28   *Fiber: 2g*
Fat: 0g   *Carbohydrates: 7g*
Protein: 1g   *Sugar: 4g*
Sodium: 200mg

SPICED BAKED TORTILLA CHIPS

PREP TIME: 5 MINUTES | COOK TIME: 15 MINUTES | SERVES 1

 Looking for a flavorful dipper to enjoy with the Chunky Guacamole, Fresh Tomato Salsa, or Pimento Cheese Spread in this chapter? These baked chips are crispy and packed with flavor and are a great way to use leftover corn tortillas in your weekly meal plan.

INGREDIENTS

2 (6") corn tortillas, cut into 8 wedges each

1 teaspoon vegetable oil

½ teaspoon fresh lime juice

¼ teaspoon chili powder

¼ teaspoon sea salt

⅛ teaspoon ground cumin

⅛ teaspoon onion powder

⅛ teaspoon garlic powder

1. Preheat oven to 350°F and line a ½ sheet pan with baking parchment.

2. In a medium bowl, add tortilla wedges, oil, and lime juice. Toss wedges well to coat, then add remaining ingredients and toss until wedges are evenly coated.

3. Place tortilla wedges in an even layer on prepared sheet pan. Bake 6–8 minutes until edges are starting to crisp, then flip and bake another 5–7 minutes until chips are golden brown and crisp. Watch chips carefully after flipping to avoid burning. Remove from oven and cool to room temperature, about 10 minutes, before enjoying.

PER SERVING

Calories: 149   Fiber: 3g
Fat: 6g   Carbohydrates: 23g
Protein: 3g   Sugar: 1g
Sodium: 430mg

PEANUT BUTTER CREAM CHEESE DIP

PREP TIME: 5 MINUTES | COOK TIME: 0 MINUTES | SERVES 1

 This indulgent peanut butter dip goes wonderfully with sliced apples, celery sticks, crackers, or pretzels. Peanut butter is a versatile pantry staple that is also used in the Soba Noodles with Peanut Sauce (Chapter 6) and Peanut Butter Banana Smoothie (Chapter 3).

INGREDIENTS

1 ounce cream cheese, softened

3 tablespoons creamy peanut butter

1 teaspoon honey

⅛ teaspoon pure vanilla extract

⅛ teaspoon ground cinnamon

¹⁄₁₆ teaspoon sea salt

In a small bowl, add cream cheese and peanut butter. With a hand mixer, beat on medium speed until well combined, about 1 minute. Add remaining ingredients and beat 30 seconds. Enjoy immediately, or cover and refrigerate for up to 3 days. Bring to room temperature before eating.

Storing Cut Apples

Extend the life of cut apples by soaking them in 1 cup water mixed with 1 teaspoon sea salt and 1 teaspoon fresh lemon juice. Let the apples soak for 5 minutes, rinse, and then store in an airtight container in the refrigerator for up to 4 days.

PER SERVING

Calories: 405   Fiber: 3g
Fat: 32g   Carbohydrates: 18g
Protein: 12g   Sugar: 12g
Sodium: 208mg

ALMOND AND CHEDDAR–STUFFED DATES

PREP TIME: 5 MINUTES | COOK TIME: 6 MINUTES | SERVES 1

 This sweet and salty snack is filling, packed with protein, and a good way to use dates in your meal plan when you have them on hand for making Apple and Brown Sugar Breakfast Cookies (Chapter 3) or Barbecue-Glazed Meatloaf (Chapter 9).

INGREDIENTS

2 tablespoons shredded sharp Cheddar cheese

⅛ teaspoon chili powder

4 pitted Medjool dates

4 whole roasted, unsalted almonds

1. Preheat oven to 350°F and line a ¼ sheet pan with baking parchment.

2. In a small bowl, combine Cheddar and chili powder. Divide mixture among dates and stuff inside. Add one almond to each date and press date closed.

3. Place dates on prepared sheet pan seam-side down. Bake 4–6 minutes until cheese is melted and dates are hot. Let cool 1 minute before enjoying.

Make a Menu Board

If you find it difficult to keep track of your meal plan day-to-day, try using a menu board. Take a small dry-erase board or chalkboard and write out the menu for the next day the night before. This keeps your meal plan top of mind!

PER SERVING

Calories: 348   Fiber: 7g

Fat: 6g   Carbohydrates: 73g

Protein: 6g   Sugar: 64g

Sodium: 99mg

TOASTED BAGUETTE WITH BRIE AND JAM

PREP TIME: 8 MINUTES | COOK TIME: 11 MINUTES | SERVES 1

 Baguette slices create a warm, toasted base for the gooey Brie cheese and sweet jam in this easy recipe. Baguettes can be sliced, stored in a freezer bag, and kept in the freezer for up to 1 month. They can also be used as a side for soups and pastas.

INGREDIENTS

2 (½"-thick) slices baguette

¼ teaspoon olive oil

1 ounce triple cream Brie cheese, rind removed

⅛ teaspoon dried thyme

⅛ teaspoon freshly cracked black pepper

4 teaspoons fig jam

2 whole roasted, unsalted almonds, chopped

1. Preheat oven to 375°F and line a ¼ sheet pan with baking parchment.

2. Place baguette slices on prepared sheet pan. Brush tops with oil. Bake 6–8 minutes until bread is starting to toast lightly and is pale in color. Remove from oven.

3. Spread Brie over tops of toast slices. Sprinkle with thyme and pepper. Top with jam and almonds.

4. Return to oven and bake 2–3 minutes until cheese is melting and jam is hot. Cool 1 minute before serving.

PER SERVING

Calories: 284   Fiber: 1g
Fat: 14g   Carbohydrates: 34g
Protein: 8g   Sugar: 14g
Sodium: 319mg

HONEY-ROASTED ALMONDS

PREP TIME: 3 MINUTES | COOK TIME: 10 MINUTES | SERVES 2

 This cook once, eat twice snack is terrific when you want something both sweet and savory in the afternoon, or something to nibble on while on the go or relaxing at home. Feel free to add an extra pinch of cayenne for a bit more heat if you like it spicy!

INGREDIENTS

1 tablespoon honey

1 cup roasted, unsalted almonds

¼ teaspoon granulated sugar

⅟₁₆ teaspoon cayenne pepper

⅟₁₆ teaspoon ground cinnamon

⅟₁₆ teaspoon sea salt

⅟₁₆ teaspoon freshly cracked black pepper

1. Preheat oven to 350°F and line a small baking sheet with baking parchment lightly sprayed with nonstick cooking spray.

2. Add all ingredients to a medium bowl. Mix, coating almonds evenly in honey and spices.

3. Spread almonds in a single layer on prepared baking sheet. Bake 6 minutes, then rotate pan and bake 3–4 minutes more until almonds have a dull shine and seasonings are very fragrant. Cool completely, about 20 minutes, on baking sheet, then transfer to an airtight container and store at room temperature for up to 2 weeks.

PER SERVING

Calories: 444   Fiber: 8g

Fat: 35g   Carbohydrates: 23g

Protein: 15g   Sugar: 12g

Sodium: 50mg

ALMOND AND DATE ENERGY BITES

PREP TIME: 10 MINUTES | COOK TIME: 0 MINUTES | SERVES 1

 These energy bites are great before or after a workout—or anytime you want a snack packed with nutrition and a bit of indulgent chocolate! You can make these up to 3 days ahead and store in the refrigerator until ready to eat.

INGREDIENTS

4 pitted Medjool dates

¼ cup hot water

1 tablespoon rolled oats

1 tablespoon almond butter

1 teaspoon honey

⅛ teaspoon ground cinnamon

2 tablespoons mini semi-sweet chocolate chips

1 tablespoon chopped roasted, unsalted almonds

1 tablespoon shredded sweetened coconut

1. In a small bowl, add dates and hot water. Let stand 10 minutes, then drain and pat dates dry with paper towel or lint-free towel.

2. Finely chop dates until they form a rough paste. Transfer back to bowl and add oats, almond butter, honey, cinnamon, and chocolate chips. Mix to combine.

3. Dampen hands with water and form mixture into three equal balls. Roll balls in almonds and coconut. Enjoy immediately or refrigerate until ready to eat, up to 3 days.

PER SERVING

Calories: 585   Fiber: 11g
Fat: 21g   Carbohydrates: 103g
Protein: 9g   Sugar: 85g
Sodium: 18mg

EVERYTHING PIGS IN A BLANKET

PREP TIME: 10 MINUTES | COOK TIME: 11 MINUTES | SERVES 1

 When you want a festive snack just for yourself, try pigs in a blanket! The cocktail sausages in this recipe can also be chopped and used in the Sausage, Egg, and Cheese Breakfast Burrito (Chapter 3) or in Cajun Chicken Pasta (Chapter 6).

INGREDIENTS

¼ cup all-purpose flour, plus extra for dusting

¼ teaspoon baking powder

⅛ teaspoon granulated sugar

2 tablespoons salted butter, cubed and chilled

1 tablespoon plus 1 teaspoon cold buttermilk

6 cocktail-sized sausages, dried well

1 tablespoon heavy whipping cream

1 teaspoon everything bagel seasoning

1. Preheat oven to 350°F and line a ¼ sheet pan with baking parchment.

2. In a medium bowl, combine flour, baking powder, and sugar. Add butter and use your fingers to rub butter into flour until mixture resembles coarse sand with some pea-sized pieces. Cover and refrigerate 10 minutes.

3. Make a well in flour mixture and add buttermilk to well. Gently stir until it just forms a shaggy ball. Turn out onto a lightly floured surface and press dough into a ¼"-thick rectangle, then fold dough in half. You may need to use a spatula or bench scraper for first few folds since dough will be shaggy. Turn dough a quarter turn and repeat this process four times. Cover dough and refrigerate 20 minutes.

4. Use your hands to form chilled dough into a ¼"-thick rectangle. Use a pizza cutter to cut dough into six strips. Wrap each strip around a sausage and place them seam-side down on prepared sheet pan. Brush tops with cream and sprinkle with everything bagel seasoning.

5. Bake 8–11 minutes until biscuits are puffed and golden brown and sausages are hot. Let cool 5 minutes before enjoying.

PER SERVING

Calories: 571	Fiber: 1g
Fat: 42g	Carbohydrates: 27g
Protein: 11g	Sugar: 2g
Sodium: 1,219mg	

CREAMY RANCH DEVILED EGGS

PREP TIME: 10 MINUTES | COOK TIME: 0 MINUTES | SERVES 2

 Deviled eggs are a protein-packed snack that make good use of eggs in your weekly meal plan. This recipe makes two servings seasoned to taste like ranch dressing. They keep for up to 4 days in the refrigerator.

INGREDIENTS

4 large hard-boiled eggs, sliced in half lengthwise

1 tablespoon mayonnaise

¼ teaspoon freeze-dried chives

¼ teaspoon freeze-dried dill

⅛ teaspoon onion powder

⅛ teaspoon garlic powder

⅛ teaspoon sea salt

⅛ teaspoon freshly cracked black pepper

⅛ teaspoon paprika

1. Gently press back of egg whites to pop egg yolks out into a small bowl along with mayonnaise. Mash with a fork until mixture is well combined and smooth. Add chives, dill, onion powder, garlic powder, salt, and pepper and mix to combine.

2. Divide filling among egg white halves. Sprinkle paprika over tops. Cover with plastic wrap and refrigerate 2 hours, up to 4 days, before serving. Enjoy chilled.

Freeze-Dried Herbs

Most well-stocked grocery stores sell freeze-dried herbs. They are most often found in the produce section with other dip mixes. If you can't find them, feel free to swap for dried herbs (using half the amount called for, as dried herbs have a more potent flavor).

PER SERVING

Calories: 202
Fat: 14g
Protein: 13g
Sodium: 265mg

Fiber: 0g
Carbohydrates: 2g
Sugar: 1g

PIZZA ROLLS

PREP TIME: 10 MINUTES | COOK TIME: 15 MINUTES | SERVES 1

 Pizza rolls are a popular way of curbing hunger between meals—and one the solo chef doesn't need to miss out on. You can divide this generous-sized snack into two servings: Simply store two of the rolls in an airtight container in the refrigerator for up to 4 days. To reheat, place them on a small baking sheet in a 350°F oven for 5–8 minutes until warmed through.

INGREDIENTS

¼ cup all-purpose flour, plus extra for dusting

¼ teaspoon baking powder

¼ teaspoon Italian seasoning

2 tablespoons salted butter, cubed and chilled

1 tablespoon plus 1 teaspoon cold buttermilk

¼ cup marinara sauce

⅓ cup shredded mozzarella cheese, divided

8 slices pepperoni

1 tablespoon grated Parmesan cheese

¼ teaspoon crushed red pepper flakes

1. Preheat oven to 350°F and spray four cups of a six-cup muffin pan with nonstick cooking spray.

2. In a medium bowl, combine flour, baking powder, and Italian seasoning. Add butter and use your fingers to rub butter into flour until mixture resembles coarse sand with some pea-sized pieces. Cover and refrigerate 10 minutes.

3. Make a well in flour mixture and add buttermilk to well. Gently stir until it just forms a shaggy ball. Turn out onto a lightly floured surface and press dough into a ¼"-thick rectangle, then fold dough in half. You may need to use a spatula or bench scraper for first few folds since dough will be shaggy. Turn dough a quarter turn and repeat this process four times. Cover dough and refrigerate 20 minutes.

4. Use your hands to form chilled dough into a ¼"-thick rectangle. Use a pizza cutter to cut dough into four strips.

5. Spread 1 tablespoon marinara over each strip. Top marinara with mozzarella, followed by 2 pepperoni slices each. Roll each strip into a roll and place them spiral-side up into prepared muffin cups. Sprinkle with Parmesan and red pepper flakes.

6. Bake 12–15 minutes or until puffed and golden brown and centers of rolls are bubbling. Let cool 5 minutes before enjoying.

PER SERVING

Calories: 531	Fiber: 1g
Fat: 34g	Carbohydrates: 31g
Protein: 16g	Sugar: 4g
Sodium: 1,028mg	

CRANBERRY BRIE MINI TARTS

PREP TIME: 10 MINUTES | COOK TIME: 10 MINUTES | SERVES 1

 Cranberry sauce adds tangy sharpness to this rich, cheesy snack. It is also found in the Cranberry Turkey Meatballs (Chapter 9), so you can add this recipe to the same week's meal plan to enjoy the cranberry sauce throughout the week!

INGREDIENTS

3 frozen mini (1.75" diameter) phyllo tart shells

1 ounce Brie cheese

1 tablespoon whole-berry cranberry sauce

1 tablespoon chopped roasted, unsalted pecans

1 teaspoon honey

⅛ teaspoon crushed red pepper flakes

1. Preheat oven to 350°F and line a ¼ sheet pan with baking parchment.

2. Place tart shells on prepared sheet pan and fill with Brie, cranberry sauce, and pecans. Bake 10 minutes or until cheese is melted and shells are golden brown around edges.

3. Remove from oven and drizzle with honey and sprinkle with red pepper flakes. Enjoy warm.

PER SERVING

Calories: 235   Fiber: 1g
Fat: 14g   Carbohydrates: 20g
Protein: 8g   Sugar: 13g
Sodium: 222mg

CHAPTER 5

SALADS, SOUPS, AND SIDES

When meal planning, it can be easy to focus solely on larger main dishes served for lunch and dinner and lose track of side dishes and lighter meals to round out your plan. But a main dish is made all the better by a complementary side dish, and not every meal calls for something heavy, complicated, and super filling.

This chapter provides one- and two-serving side dishes to pair with main dishes later in this book, as well as lighter meals like soups and salads you can add to your meal plan for lunches and dinners. For example, you can make the cook once, eat twice recipe for Twice-Baked Potato with Broccoli and enjoy one as a side dish with Seared Beef Filet with Herb Butter (Chapter 9) one evening and reheat the second for lunch later in the week paired with a Chopped House Salad with Ranch (in this chapter). Or try the Creamy Asparagus Soup for a lighter meal, and use the leftover asparagus to make Roasted Asparagus with Lemon and Parmesan to serve with Parchment-Baked Salmon (Chapter 8). A little planning goes a long way toward a satisfying weekly meal plan you truly look forward to!

CREAMY ASPARAGUS SOUP

PREP TIME: 10 MINUTES | COOK TIME: 16 MINUTES | SERVES 1

 This fresh summer soup is delicious paired with the Chopped House Salad with Ranch in this chapter. Add it to your meal plans that also include Roasted Asparagus with Lemon and Parmesan (this chapter) or Asparagus Risotto (Chapter 7).

INGREDIENTS

2 teaspoons salted butter

1 teaspoon olive oil

½ pound asparagus, trimmed and cut into ½" pieces

2 tablespoons finely chopped yellow onion

½ clove garlic, peeled and minced

¼ teaspoon Italian seasoning

⅛ teaspoon sea salt

⅛ teaspoon freshly cracked black pepper

½ cup low-sodium vegetable broth

1 tablespoon heavy whipping cream

¼ teaspoon freeze-dried chives

1. In a small pot over medium heat, add butter and oil. Once butter is melted, swirl pot to evenly coat, then add asparagus. Sauté 3 minutes, then add onion and sauté 1 minute or until onion is starting to turn translucent.

2. Add garlic, Italian seasoning, salt, and pepper to pot and cook until garlic and spices are fragrant, about 30 seconds. Add broth and scrape bottom of pot to release any bits stuck to bottom.

3. Bring soup to a boil over medium heat, then reduce heat to low and simmer 10 minutes or until asparagus is very tender. Transfer mixture to a blender, or use an immersion blender, and purée until very smooth, about 1 minute.

4. Once smooth, return to pot and stir in cream and chives. Let stand on low heat 1 minute. Serve hot.

PER SERVING

Calories: 207 Fiber: 4g

Fat: 17g Carbohydrates: 11g

Protein: 5g Sugar: 6g

Sodium: 333mg

TRADITIONAL POTATO SALAD

PREP TIME: 5 MINUTES | COOK TIME: 10 MINUTES | SERVES 2

 This cook once, eat twice side dish keeps for 5 days in the refrigerator and is a tasty addition to meal plans that also include Crispy Fried Shrimp (Chapter 8), Peach-Glazed Pork Chop (Chapter 9), or Baked Cheeseburger Sliders (Chapter 9).

INGREDIENTS

1 (6-ounce) russet potato, peeled and cut into ½" pieces

1 large hard-boiled egg, chopped

2 tablespoons mayonnaise

½ teaspoon yellow mustard

1 tablespoon minced yellow onion

1 tablespoon minced celery

1 teaspoon dill pickle relish

¼ teaspoon sea salt

⅛ teaspoon freshly cracked black pepper

1 In a small pot, add potato and enough water to cover potato by ½". Heat over medium-high heat and bring to a boil. Reduce heat to medium and cook until potato pieces are fork-tender, about 10 minutes. Drain potato and let cool 10 minutes.

2 Add remaining ingredients to a medium bowl and mix well to combine.

3 Add cooled potato to dressing and fold to combine. Cover bowl and refrigerate at least 2 hours, up to 5 days. Serve chilled.

Lighten It Up!

If you want to lighten up this potato salad—or any mayonnaise-based salad dressing—swap all or at least half the mayonnaise for an equal amount of 2% Greek yogurt. Yogurt is just as creamy, has a tangy flavor, and can also be used for breakfast in your weekly meal plan!

PER SERVING

Calories: 204   Fiber: 2g

Fat: 12g   Carbohydrates: 17g

Protein: 5g   Sugar: 1g

Sodium: 361mg

ROASTED ASPARAGUS WITH LEMON AND PARMESAN

PREP TIME: 5 MINUTES | COOK TIME: 20 MINUTES | SERVES 1

 This elegant side dish is ideal when served with seafood, fish, or roasted meat dishes. Some ideas for meal plan pairing include Garlic Scampi (Chapter 8), Seared Beef Filet with Herb Butter, or Braised Beef Short Rib (both in Chapter 9).

INGREDIENTS

¼ pound asparagus, ends trimmed

1 teaspoon olive oil

⅛ teaspoon sea salt

⅛ teaspoon freshly cracked black pepper

1 teaspoon fresh lemon zest

1 tablespoon grated Parmesan cheese

1. Preheat oven to 400°F and line a ¼ sheet pan with baking parchment.

2. Add asparagus to prepared sheet pan. Drizzle with oil and toss to coat. Sprinkle with salt and pepper and toss to distribute.

3. Spread asparagus into an even layer. Sprinkle lemon zest and Parmesan over top. Bake 18–20 minutes until asparagus is tender yet still crisp. Serve immediately.

PER SERVING

Calories: 82   Fiber: 3g

Fat: 6g   Carbohydrates: 6g

Protein: 4g   Sugar: 2g

Sodium: 287mg

BUTTERY HERB RICE

PREP TIME: 5 MINUTES | COOK TIME: 18 MINUTES | SERVES 1

 Rice is a pantry staple that makes for an easy and flavorful side dish for meats, seafoods, and roasted vegetables. This rice dish is flavored with herbs and butter, but for even more flavor, you can make it with chicken broth instead of water.

INGREDIENTS

¼ cup uncooked medium-grain white rice, rinsed and drained

½ cup water

1 tablespoon salted butter, divided

¼ teaspoon dried thyme

¼ teaspoon freeze-dried chives

½ teaspoon fresh lemon zest

⅛ teaspoon garlic powder

⅛ teaspoon onion powder

⅛ teaspoon sea salt

1. In a 1-quart saucepan over medium heat, add rice, water, 1 teaspoon butter, thyme, chives, lemon zest, garlic powder, onion powder, and salt. Cover pot and heat until mixture comes to a boil.

2. Once boiling, reduce heat to low and cook 16–18 minutes until liquid is fully absorbed and rice is tender. Remove pan from heat and let stand covered 10 minutes.

3. Uncover rice and fluff. Add remaining 2 teaspoons butter and fold to combine. Serve hot.

Plain Rice
To make plain white rice, just make this as directed but swap butter for ½ teaspoon vegetable oil and omit the thyme, chives, lemon zest, garlic powder, and onion powder. Cook as directed and fluff before serving.

PER SERVING

Calories: 284
Fat: 11g
Protein: 4g
Sodium: 286mg

Fiber: 1g
Carbohydrates: 41g
Sugar: 0g

WHIPPED YUKON GOLD POTATO WITH CHIVES

PREP TIME: 10 MINUTES | COOK TIME: 11 MINUTES | SERVES 1

 Whipped potatoes are a bit lighter than traditional mashed potatoes and scrumptiously smooth and creamy. When making your weekly meal plan, consider this side along with braised or roasted meats such as Braised Beef Short Rib (Chapter 9) or Beef Short Rib Pot Roast (Chapter 9).

INGREDIENTS

1 (6-ounce) Yukon Gold potato, peeled and cut into ½" cubes

1 teaspoon sea salt, divided

¼ cup heavy whipping cream

½ teaspoon freeze-dried chives

3 teaspoons salted butter

⅛ teaspoon garlic powder

⅛ teaspoon onion powder

⅛ teaspoon freshly cracked black pepper

1 Place potato in a small pot. Add enough water to cover potato by ½" and sprinkle with ½ teaspoon salt. Heat over medium-high heat and bring to a boil. Reduce heat to medium and cook until potato is fork-tender, about 10 minutes. Drain potato and return to hot pot.

2 While potato cooks, combine cream and chives in a small bowl and warm 30 seconds on high in microwave, or until cream is warm.

3 Add butter to pot with potato. Mix with a hand mixer on low speed until potato cubes are broken down into smaller pieces, then add warmed cream, remaining ½ teaspoon salt, garlic powder, onion powder, and pepper. Increase speed to high and beat until potato mixture is smooth and lighter in texture, about 45–50 seconds. Serve hot.

Make Potatoes Ahead

Whipped potatoes can be made up to 5 days ahead. To reheat, place potatoes in a microwave-safe bowl and heat on high 45 seconds. Stir and continue to heat in 30-second intervals, stirring between each, until steaming hot. Add 1–2 teaspoons of heavy whipping cream if potatoes seem too thick.

PER SERVING

Calories: 442
Fat: 32g
Protein: 4g
Sodium: 1,268mg

Fiber: 3g
Carbohydrates: 34g
Sugar: 3g

SAFFRON RICE

PREP TIME: 5 MINUTES | COOK TIME: 18 MINUTES | SERVES 1

 Looking for an easy side dish to pair with Chickpea Masala (Chapter 7) or Parchment-Baked Salmon (Chapter 8)? This fragrant rice is wonderful for heavily spiced meals or light fish and seafood dishes in your weekly meal plan.

INGREDIENTS

¼ cup uncooked medium-grain white rice, rinsed and drained

½ cup low-sodium vegetable broth

1 teaspoon olive oil

⅛ teaspoon saffron threads, crushed

⅛ teaspoon ground cumin

⅛ teaspoon garlic powder

⅛ teaspoon onion powder

⅛ teaspoon sea salt

1. Add all ingredients to a 1-quart saucepan over medium heat and stir well. Cover pot and heat until mixture comes to a boil.

2. Once boiling, reduce heat to low and cook 16–18 minutes until liquid is fully absorbed and rice is tender. Remove pan from heat and let stand covered 10 minutes.

3. Uncover rice and fluff. Serve hot.

Swap for Saffron

Saffron can be pretty expensive, so if you want to swap it for something more affordable, you can use ⅛ teaspoon ground turmeric. It will provide a pretty yellow color and a mild, earthy flavor without the bigger price tag.

PER SERVING

Calories: 233   Fiber: 1g
Fat: 5g   Carbohydrates: 43g
Protein: 4g   Sugar: 2g
Sodium: 265mg

VEGETARIAN CHARRO BEANS

PREP TIME: 10 MINUTES | COOK TIME: 12 MINUTES | SERVES 2

 This quick and easy charro bean recipe is ready in a flash and makes enough to enjoy a second serving later in the week. If you like, you can add 2 tablespoons chopped Canadian bacon along with the diced tomato to add even more flavor! If you want these beans to be more like soup, add more broth during Step 2 when simmering.

INGREDIENTS

1 teaspoon vegetable oil

2 tablespoons minced yellow onion

1 medium Roma tomato, seeded and diced

½ clove garlic, peeled and minced

¼ teaspoon ground cumin

¼ teaspoon chili powder

3 tablespoons chopped fresh cilantro

1 (15-ounce) can pinto beans, drained and rinsed

1 cup low-sodium vegetable broth

¼ teaspoon sea salt

1. In a small pot over medium heat, add oil. Once hot, add onion and tomato and sauté 1 minute. Add garlic, cumin, and chili powder and cook until very fragrant, about 1 minute, then add cilantro and stir well.

2. Add beans and broth to pot and stir well. Bring to a boil over medium heat, then reduce heat to low and simmer 10 minutes, stirring often. After 10 minutes, check texture. If you want your beans thicker, continue simmering until desired consistency is reached.

3. Season with salt. Serve hot. Additional portion can be refrigerated for up to 5 days.

PER SERVING

Calories: 195   Fiber: 1g
Fat: 2g   Carbohydrates: 32g
Protein: 10g   Sugar: 3g
Sodium: 550mg

SEVEN LAYER SALAD

PREP TIME: 10 MINUTES | COOK TIME: 0 MINUTES | SERVES 1

 This single-portion take on the potluck classic makes it easy to enjoy a hearty salad on your meal plan without having enough to feed an army. Make this in a resealable container or wide-mouthed jar with a lid if you plan to make it and take it for lunch!

INGREDIENTS

1 tablespoon sour cream

1 tablespoon mayonnaise

¼ teaspoon fresh lemon juice

¹⁄₁₆ teaspoon Worcestershire sauce

⅛ teaspoon freshly cracked black pepper

2 cups lightly packed fresh baby spinach

1 large hard-boiled egg, sliced

1 cup shredded iceberg lettuce

2 strips bacon, cooked crisp and crumbled

1 green onion, green part only, chopped

¼ cup frozen peas

2 tablespoons shredded sharp Cheddar cheese

1. In a small bowl, add sour cream, mayonnaise, lemon juice, Worcestershire sauce, and pepper. Mix well. Set aside.

2. In a serving bowl, layer spinach, egg, lettuce, bacon, green onion, and peas. Spread dressing over top of salad. Cover and refrigerate at least 4 hours, up to overnight.

3. To serve, top dressing with Cheddar. Serve chilled.

PER SERVING

Calories: 306   Fiber: 3g
Fat: 23g   Carbohydrates: 7g
Protein: 16g   Sugar: 3g
Sodium: 537mg

MACARONI SALAD

PREP TIME: 10 MINUTES | COOK TIME: 10 MINUTES | SERVES 1

 This single portion of a summer favorite is perfect for enjoying with Baked Cheeseburger Sliders (Chapter 9) or Crispy Fried Shrimp (Chapter 8). It tastes better with time, so feel free to make it up to 4 days ahead.

INGREDIENTS

2 ounces dried elbow macaroni

½ teaspoon sea salt, divided

2 tablespoons mayonnaise

1 teaspoon Dijon mustard

¼ teaspoon granulated sugar

⅛ teaspoon freshly cracked black pepper

¼ cup finely chopped celery

¼ cup finely chopped red bell pepper

1 tablespoon finely chopped yellow onion

⅛ teaspoon paprika

1. In a 2-quart saucepan over high heat, add water to fill pot ¾ full. Once water begins to boil, add macaroni and ¼ teaspoon salt. Cook, stirring occasionally, until pasta is al dente, about 10 minutes. Rinse with cold running water to cool pasta.

2. While pasta cooks, combine remaining ¼ teaspoon salt, mayonnaise, mustard, sugar, and black pepper in a medium bowl. Add the celery, bell pepper, and onion and mix.

3. Once pasta is ready, add to mayonnaise mixture and fold to combine. Sprinkle with paprika. Cover and refrigerate at least 2 hours, up to 4 days. Serve chilled.

PER SERVING

Calories: 439 *Fiber: 4g*
Fat: 22g *Carbohydrates: 49g*
Protein: 10g *Sugar: 4g*
Sodium: 894mg

HONEY-GLAZED CARROTS

PREP TIME: 5 MINUTES | COOK TIME: 13 MINUTES | SERVES 1

 Glazed carrots make a wonderful fall or winter side dish, and leftover carrots can be used in soups and stews or eaten as a snack during the week with a dip, such as the Chunky Guacamole in Chapter 4.

INGREDIENTS

⅓ cup water

4 ounces baby carrots

2 teaspoons unsalted butter

2 teaspoons honey

⅛ teaspoon ground cinnamon

⅛ teaspoon sea salt

⅛ teaspoon freshly cracked black pepper

1. In a 2-quart saucepan over medium heat, add water and bring to a simmer. Add carrots, cover, and cook 10 minutes or until carrots are fork-tender. Drain and return to pot.

2. Add remaining ingredients to pot and return to medium heat. Cook, stirring frequently, until carrots are thickly coated in glaze, about 3 minutes. Serve warm.

PER SERVING

Calories: 155   Fiber: 3g
Fat: 7g   Carbohydrates: 23g
Protein: 1g   Sugar: 17g
Sodium: 274mg

ROASTED BROCCOLI

PREP TIME: 10 MINUTES | COOK TIME: 20 MINUTES | SERVES 1

 This is a tasty and easy side to fish dishes like Pan-Fried Trout with Lemon Butter (Chapter 8). If you want to use more broccoli in your weekly meal plan, try the Pasta Primavera (Chapter 6) or the Twice-Baked Potato with Broccoli in this chapter.

INGREDIENTS

1½ cups broccoli florets

1 tablespoon olive oil

⅛ teaspoon freshly cracked black pepper

⅛ teaspoon sea salt

1 clove garlic, peeled and roughly chopped

2 tablespoons finely minced yellow onion

½ teaspoon fresh lemon zest

2 tablespoons grated Parmesan cheese

1. Preheat oven to 425°F and line a ¼ sheet pan with aluminum foil.

2. Place broccoli on prepared sheet pan and drizzle with oil. Toss gently to mix, then sprinkle with pepper and salt.

3. Bake 10 minutes, then add garlic and onion, stir, and flip broccoli. Bake 8–10 minutes more until broccoli stems are tender.

4. Remove from oven and sprinkle with lemon zest and Parmesan. Serve immediately.

PER SERVING

Calories: 219   Fiber: 4g

Fat: 16g   Carbohydrates: 14g

Protein: 7g   Sugar: 3g

Sodium: 420mg

CREAMY MUSHROOM SOUP

PREP TIME: 5 MINUTES | COOK TIME: 33 MINUTES | SERVES 1

 White miso paste adds intense depth of flavor to this soup, and leftover paste can be whisked into marinades and dressings for added umami. Miso is also used in Sesame Garlic Soba Noodles (Chapter 6) and Miso-Glazed Salmon (Chapter 8).

INGREDIENTS

1 tablespoon salted butter

4 ounces sliced button mushrooms

¼ cup chopped yellow onion

1 clove garlic, peeled and chopped

⅛ teaspoon dried thyme

⅛ teaspoon Italian seasoning

1 cup low-sodium vegetable broth

2 teaspoons white miso paste

2 tablespoons heavy whipping cream

¼ teaspoon sea salt

¼ teaspoon freshly cracked black pepper

1. In a 2-quart pot over medium heat, add butter. Once melted, swirl to coat bottom of pot and add mushrooms. Cook, stirring occasionally, until mushrooms are golden brown and tender, about 8 minutes.

2. Add onion and cook 3 minutes, then add garlic, thyme, and Italian seasoning and cook 30 seconds. Add broth, scraping any bits from bottom of pot, and bring to a boil over medium heat. Once boiling, reduce heat to low, cover, and simmer 20 minutes.

3. Remove lid and stir soup. Turn off heat and stir in miso paste. Transfer soup to a blender, or use an immersion blender, and purée until smooth, about 30 seconds.

4. Return to pot and stir in cream, salt, and pepper. Cook 1 minute over medium-low heat to warm cream. Serve hot.

Shelf Life of Miso

As a preserved food, miso has a long shelf life. If kept refrigerated in an airtight container, it can last for 6 months. Be sure to keep plastic wrap or wax paper pressed against the miso to keep it from drying out.

PER SERVING

Calories: 186

Fat: 12g

Protein: 6g

Sodium: 1,098mg

Fiber: 4g

Carbohydrates: 15g

Sugar: 8g

POTATOES AU GRATIN

PREP TIME: 10 MINUTES | COOK TIME: 1 HOUR 5 MINUTES | SERVES 1

 If you have Seared Beef Filet with Herb Butter (Chapter 9) or any roasted or braised meat on the menu, then you should add this creamy, cheesy side to your meal plan! Extra Yukon Gold potatoes can be used in the Whipped Yukon Gold Potato with Chives in this chapter.

INGREDIENTS

½ cup heavy whipping cream

1 clove garlic, peeled and minced

¼ teaspoon sea salt

¼ teaspoon freshly cracked black pepper

⅛ teaspoon dried thyme

¼ teaspoon cornstarch

1 (6-ounce) Yukon Gold potato, peeled and thinly sliced

⅓ cup shredded sharp Cheddar cheese

1. In a small saucepan over medium heat, add cream, garlic, salt, pepper, and thyme. Bring to a simmer, about 5 minutes, then remove from heat and whisk in cornstarch. Set aside.

2. In a 6" baking dish sprayed with nonstick cooking spray, layer ⅓ of potato slices. Spoon ⅓ of cream mixture on top and sprinkle ⅓ of Cheddar. Repeat layers twice more.

3. Cover dish tightly with aluminum foil and bake 50 minutes, then uncover and bake 10 minutes to brown cheese. Remove from oven and let stand 10 minutes before serving.

PER SERVING

Calories: 713
Fat: 53g
Protein: 15g
Sodium: 684mg

Fiber: 3g
Carbohydrates: 39g
Sugar: 6g

MEDITERRANEAN PASTA SALAD

PREP TIME: 10 MINUTES | COOK TIME: 10 MINUTES | SERVES 2

 You get two servings of this fresh and flavorful pasta salad to enjoy for lunches and dinners in your weekly meal plan! The feta used in this recipe is also used in the Spinach and Feta–Stuffed Mushroom in Chapter 7.

INGREDIENTS

4 ounces dried rotini pasta

¾ teaspoon sea salt, divided

⅓ cup chopped red bell pepper

⅓ cup chopped English cucumber

⅓ cup sliced cherry tomatoes

¼ medium red onion, peeled and sliced

6 pitted kalamata olives, sliced

2 tablespoons crumbled feta cheese

2 tablespoons chopped fresh Italian parsley

2 tablespoons olive oil

1 teaspoon fresh lemon juice

⅛ teaspoon garlic powder

⅛ teaspoon freshly cracked black pepper

1. In a 2-quart saucepan over high heat, add water to fill pot ¾ full. Once water begins to boil, add pasta and ½ teaspoon salt. Cook, stirring occasionally, until pasta is al dente, about 10 minutes. Rinse with cold running water to cool pasta.

2. Add cooled pasta to a medium bowl along with bell pepper, cucumber, tomatoes, onion, olives, feta, and parsley. Toss to mix.

3. In a small bowl, whisk together oil, lemon juice, garlic powder, black pepper, and remaining ¼ teaspoon salt. Pour mixture over pasta and toss to evenly coat. Cover and refrigerate at least 2 hours, up to 3 days. Serve chilled or at room temperature.

PER SERVING

Calories: 410   Fiber: 4g
Fat: 19g   Carbohydrates: 48g
Protein: 10g   Sugar: 4g
Sodium: 640mg

CHOPPED HOUSE SALAD WITH RANCH

PREP TIME: 15 MINUTES | COOK TIME: 0 MINUTES | SERVES 1

 This salad is hearty enough to be a meal on its own for lunch or a lighter dinner. The remaining iceberg lettuce can be used in your meal plan as a topping for a Mushroom Gyro (Chapter 7) or Shrimp Po' Boy (Chapter 8).

INGREDIENTS

2 tablespoons sour cream

1 tablespoon heavy whipping cream

⅛ teaspoon onion powder

⅛ teaspoon garlic powder

¼ teaspoon freeze-dried chives

¼ teaspoon freeze-dried dill

¼ teaspoon freshly cracked black pepper

⅛ teaspoon sea salt

2 cups chopped romaine lettuce

1 cup chopped iceberg lettuce

¼ cup sliced cherry tomatoes

¼ cup chopped English cucumber

2 tablespoons chopped red onion

1 large hard-boiled egg, chopped

2 tablespoons chopped cooked bacon

2 tablespoons shredded sharp Cheddar cheese

1. In a small bowl, combine sour cream, cream, onion powder, and garlic powder. Add chives, dill, pepper, and salt. Mix well, then cover and refrigerate at least 1 hour, up to 5 days.

2. In a serving bowl, add romaine and iceberg lettuces and toss to combine. Add tomatoes, cucumber, and onion and toss gently to mix. Top salad with egg, bacon, and Cheddar. Drizzle with prepared dressing. Serve immediately.

PER SERVING

Calories: 362 | Fat: 24g | Protein: 20g | Sodium: 702mg | Fiber: 4g Carbohydrates: 12g | Sugar: 7g

TWICE-BAKED POTATO WITH BROCCOLI

PREP TIME: 15 MINUTES | COOK TIME: 1 HOUR 35 MINUTES | SERVES 2

 Twice-baked potatoes are a starch and vegetable side all in one on your weekly meal plan. To reheat the second serving, you can microwave it on high for 3 minutes or until steaming hot, or bake it at 350°F for 10–15 minutes.

INGREDIENTS

1 (8-ounce) russet potato, scrubbed and dried

¼ teaspoon olive oil

⅓ cup chopped fresh broccoli

2 tablespoons water

2 tablespoons sour cream

1 tablespoon salted butter

1 tablespoon heavy whipping cream

¼ teaspoon sea salt

¼ teaspoon freshly cracked black pepper

⅛ teaspoon onion powder

⅛ teaspoon garlic powder

¼ cup shredded sharp Cheddar cheese

¼ teaspoon smoked paprika

PER SERVING

Calories: 277   *Fiber: 3g*
Fat: 15g   *Carbohydrates: 27g*
Protein: 7g   *Sugar: 2g*
Sodium: 359mg

1. Preheat oven to 400°F.

2. With a paring knife, poke six holes into potato, three on each side. Rub skin with oil.

3. Place potato directly on oven rack and bake 60–70 minutes until a paring knife slips easily in and out of potato flesh. Remove from oven and let cool 15 minutes.

4. Reduce oven to 350°F.

5. While potato is baking, add broccoli and water to a small microwave-safe bowl. Cover bowl with a lid or plastic wrap and microwave on high 3 minutes. Remove from microwave and drain off excess water. Set aside.

6. Slice cooled potato in half lengthwise. Scoop potato flesh, leaving about ¼" of flesh in skin, into a small bowl. Add sour cream, butter, cream, salt, pepper, onion powder, and garlic powder. Mix well, stirring until mixture is well combined. Fold in broccoli.

7. Divide mixture between hollowed-out potato skins. Top with Cheddar and sprinkle with paprika. Bake 20–25 minutes until cheese is melted and starting to bubble. Cool 5 minutes before serving. Cool the second potato for 20 minutes at room temperature, then place in an airtight container and refrigerate for up to 5 days.

CHICKEN NOODLE SOUP

PREP TIME: 10 MINUTES | COOK TIME: 24 MINUTES | SERVES 1

 You can use any shape of pasta for this soup, so feel free to swap in what you have on hand when building your meal plan. For a spicy kick, add in a fat pinch (about ⅛ teaspoon) crushed red pepper flakes with the salt and pepper. You can make this up to 5 days ahead and store in the refrigerator. Reheat in microwave for 3–5 minutes on high until steamy hot.

INGREDIENTS

2 teaspoons olive oil

3 tablespoons chopped yellow onion

3 tablespoons chopped celery

2 tablespoons chopped carrot

¼ teaspoon sea salt

¼ teaspoon freshly cracked black pepper

¼ teaspoon poultry seasoning

2 cups low-sodium chicken broth

1 (4-ounce) boneless, skinless chicken breast

1 ounce dried rotini pasta

¼ teaspoon fresh lemon juice

1. In a 2-quart saucepan over high heat, add oil. Once hot, swirl pan to coat bottom and add onion, celery, and carrot. Cook until tender, about 5 minutes. Add salt, pepper, and poultry seasoning and cook until spices are fragrant, about 30 seconds.

2. Add broth to pan and stir well, then add chicken. Bring mixture to a boil, then reduce heat to low, cover pan, and cook 10 minutes or until chicken reaches an internal temperature of 160°F in thickest part.

3. Remove chicken from pan and let cool slightly, about 3 minutes, then shred with two forks. Set aside.

4. While chicken cools, return pan to medium heat and add pasta. Cook until pasta is tender, about 8 minutes. Reduce heat to low and add shredded chicken and lemon juice. Stir, then serve hot.

PER SERVING

Calories: 350   Fiber: 3g

Fat: 12g   Carbohydrates: 27g

Protein: 33g   Sugar: 3g

Sodium: 744mg

QUICK BLACK BEAN SOUP

PREP TIME: 10 MINUTES | COOK TIME: 15 MINUTES | SERVES 1

 This soup is ready in a flash when you want quick comfort food. To use up the extra black beans, tomato, and cilantro, add the Black Bean Tacos with Corn and Tomato Relish in Chapter 7 to the same meal plan as this soup.

INGREDIENTS

1 teaspoon olive oil

2 tablespoons finely chopped yellow onion

2 slices Canadian bacon, chopped

¼ cup chopped Roma tomato

½ clove garlic, peeled and minced

¼ teaspoon ground cumin

⅛ teaspoon sea salt

⅛ teaspoon freshly cracked black pepper

½ (15-ounce) can black beans, drained and rinsed

1½ cups low-sodium vegetable broth

1 tablespoon chopped fresh cilantro

1. In a 2-quart saucepan over high heat, add oil. Once hot, swirl pan to coat bottom and add onion. Cook until just tender, about 3 minutes. Add Canadian bacon and tomato and cook until tomato is very soft, about 3 minutes.

2. Add garlic, cumin, salt, and pepper and cook until garlic is fragrant, about 30 seconds. Add beans, broth, and cilantro and stir well. Bring to a boil, then reduce heat to medium-low and simmer 5–8 minutes until cilantro is fragrant. Serve hot.

Track Leftover Ingredients

Be sure to keep track of leftover ingredients when you plan your weekly meals. Recipes for one will often leave leftover vegetables or canned items. Keep track of those quantities when planning so you can use them up in other recipes, or in the following week's meal plan!

PER SERVING

Calories: 287 *Fiber: 16g*
Fat: 6g *Carbohydrates: 40g*
Protein: 20g *Sugar: 3g*
Sodium: 925mg

CHAPTER 6

PASTA AND NOODLE DISHES

Pasta is a real hero in the solo meal planning pantry! When you have a busy day, meal planning for a one-pot pasta dish means dinner is just a few moments away. Additionally, there is usually minimal cleanup involved. On days when you have more time to spend in the kitchen, you can plan for more leisurely baked pasta dishes that are as comforting as they are yummy. Because pasta is versatile, you can enjoy a variety of cuisines and flavors, so pasta night never has to be boring. Some pasta dishes also make good leftovers, so you can cook once and eat twice without sacrificing taste.

This chapter explores pasta and noodle dishes in single and double servings, with recipes ranging from fresh and light to rich and creamy. When time is tight, you have loads of options that will be ready in under 20 minutes, including Garlic Butter Shrimp Pasta and Creamy Pesto Ravioli. For a lighter meal, try the Sesame Garlic Soba Noodles or the Pasta Primavera. And when comfort is what you crave, look no further than the Baked Macaroni and Cheese for One or the Cacio e Pepe. These recipes will round out your meal plan in an easy, delectable way!

ITALIAN ROTINI SALAD

PREP TIME: 10 MINUTES | COOK TIME: 8 MINUTES | SERVES 2

 Cook once, eat twice Italian Rotini Salad is great for lunch one day and a light dinner the next. When planning for the week, remember that the pimentos used here can also be used in Pimento Cheese Spread (Chapter 4).

INGREDIENTS

4 ounces dried rotini pasta

½ teaspoon sea salt

1 tablespoon olive oil

2 teaspoons red wine vinegar

1 teaspoon basil pesto

⅓ cup whole pitted black olives

⅓ cup whole cherry tomatoes

¼ cup chopped red onion

¼ cup shredded Parmesan cheese

3 tablespoons drained diced pimentos

1. In a 2-quart pot over high heat, add water to fill pot ¾ full. Once water begins to boil, add pasta and salt. Cook, stirring occasionally, until pasta is just al dente, about 8 minutes. Reserve ½ cup pasta water, then drain pasta and run under cool water to stop cooking. Set aside to drain.

2. In a medium bowl, add oil, vinegar, and pesto and whisk well. Add pasta and remaining ingredients and toss to coat. If pasta sauce seems dry, stir in reserved pasta water 1 tablespoon at a time until sauce loosens. Cover and refrigerate at least 2 hours, up to 4 days. Serve chilled or at room temperature.

PER SERVING

Calories: 381   Fiber: 4g

Fat: 14g   Carbohydrates: 50g

Protein: 13g   Sugar: 3g

Sodium: 602mg

BAKED ROTINI WITH RICOTTA

PREP TIME: 10 MINUTES | COOK TIME: 38 MINUTES | SERVES 1

 This indulgent dish is ready for the oven in less than 20 minutes and ready for the table about 30 minutes later! The leftover ricotta can be used for breakfast the next day if you add Honey Ricotta Toast with Fresh Strawberries to your meal plan.

INGREDIENTS

¾ teaspoon sea salt, divided

2 ounces dried rotini pasta

½ cup canned crushed tomatoes, undrained

½ teaspoon Italian seasoning

⅛ teaspoon garlic powder

¼ cup whole milk ricotta cheese

2 tablespoons grated Parmesan cheese

⅛ teaspoon crushed red pepper flakes

1. Preheat oven to 375°F and spray a 6" baking dish with nonstick cooking spray.

2. In a 2-quart saucepan over high heat, add water to fill pot ¾ full. Once water begins to boil, add pasta and ½ teaspoon salt. Cook, stirring occasionally, until pasta is just under al dente, about 8 minutes. Reserve ¼ cup pasta water. Drain well.

3. Add tomatoes, Italian seasoning, garlic powder, and remaining ¼ teaspoon salt to a medium bowl and mix well. Add pasta to sauce along with reserved pasta water and toss to coat.

4. Transfer pasta and sauce to prepared dish. Add ricotta to the top by heaping teaspoons over pasta, then sprinkle on Parmesan and red pepper flakes.

5. Bake 25–30 minutes until mixture is bubbling around edges. Cool 5 minutes before serving.

PER SERVING

Calories: 414
Fat: 11g
Protein: 20g
Sodium: 1,065mg

Fiber: 6g
Carbohydrates: 56g
Sugar: 5g

BAKED MACARONI AND CHEESE FOR ONE

PREP TIME: 10 MINUTES | COOK TIME: 36 MINUTES | SERVES 1

 This is pure comfort food and can be made with any tube- or spiral-shaped pasta you have in your pantry. If you need a way to use the extra milk from this recipe, add the Crispy Fried Shrimp or Shrimp and Grits (both in Chapter 8) to your meal plan!

INGREDIENTS

½ teaspoon sea salt, divided

2 ounces dried elbow macaroni

1 tablespoon salted butter

1 tablespoon all-purpose flour

¼ teaspoon freshly cracked black pepper

⅛ teaspoon dried mustard powder

⅛ teaspoon onion powder

⅔ cup whole milk

½ cup shredded sharp Cheddar cheese

1 tablespoon grated Parmesan cheese

⅛ teaspoon smoked paprika

1. Preheat oven to 375°F and spray a 1-quart baking dish with nonstick cooking spray.

2. In a 2-quart saucepan over high heat, add water to fill pot ¾ full. Once water begins to boil, add ¼ teaspoon salt and macaroni. Cook, stirring occasionally, until pasta is just under al dente, about 8 minutes. Drain and set aside.

3. Return pot to medium heat and add butter. Once melted and foaming, add flour, pepper, mustard powder, and onion powder. Whisk to combine and cook 45 seconds, then slowly whisk in milk. Cook, whisking constantly, until sauce starts to bubble and thicken, about 2 minutes.

4. Turn off heat and add Cheddar. Whisk until cheese is melted, then fold in cooked pasta.

5. Transfer pasta to prepared dish. Top with remaining ¼ teaspoon salt, Parmesan, and paprika. Bake 20–25 minutes until edges of dish are bubbling and top is golden brown. Cool 5 minutes before enjoying.

PER SERVING

Calories: 700
Fat: 34g
Protein: 29g
Sodium: 1,186mg

Fiber: 3g
Carbohydrates: 59g
Sugar: 9g

RAVIOLI LASAGNA

PREP TIME: 10 MINUTES | COOK TIME: 52 MINUTES | SERVES 2

 This cook once, eat twice layered ravioli dish makes a terrific lunch or dinner in your weekly meal plan. To reheat the second portion, either bake it at 350°F for 10–12 minutes or microwave it on high for 1–2 minutes until hot. Add a side of warm bread or a refreshing salad.

INGREDIENTS

1 cup canned crushed tomatoes, undrained

¼ teaspoon garlic powder

¼ teaspoon onion powder

¼ teaspoon Italian seasoning

12 frozen large cheese ravioli

½ cup shredded mozzarella cheese

¼ cup grated Parmesan cheese

1. Preheat oven to 400°F and spray a 1-quart baking dish with nonstick cooking spray.

2. In a small bowl, add tomatoes, garlic powder, onion powder, and Italian seasoning. Mix well.

3. Spread ⅓ of tomato sauce into prepared dish. Top with an even layer of 4 ravioli, followed by ⅓ mozzarella and ⅓ Parmesan. Repeat layers, ending with mozzarella and Parmesan.

4. Cover dish tightly with aluminum foil and bake 40 minutes. Uncover and bake 10–12 minutes more until cheese is golden brown on top and bubbling. Cool 10 minutes before serving.

PER SERVING

Calories: 488   Fiber: 5g
Fat: 14g   Carbohydrates: 65g
Protein: 24g   Sugar: 7g
Sodium: 1,004mg

SPAGHETTI WITH TANGY TOMATO SAUCE

PREP TIME: 10 MINUTES | COOK TIME: 17 MINUTES | SERVES 1

 Fresh tomato, crushed tomato, and tomato paste give the sauce its rich flavor in this recipe. Add a portion of Beef and Pork Meatballs (Chapter 9) to your meal plan to make this pasta dish even heartier and more filling.

INGREDIENTS

1 teaspoon olive oil

1 clove garlic, peeled

2 tablespoons finely chopped yellow onion

1 teaspoon tomato paste

⅓ cup diced Roma tomato

⅓ cup canned crushed tomatoes, undrained

¼ teaspoon Italian seasoning

2 ounces dried spaghetti pasta

¼ teaspoon salt

2 tablespoons grated Parmesan cheese

1 tablespoon chopped fresh basil

1. In a small saucepan over medium heat, add oil. Once hot, add garlic, onion, and tomato paste and cook, stirring constantly, until very fragrant, about 1 minute. Add Roma tomato and cook until tender, about 1 minute.

2. Add crushed tomatoes and Italian seasoning to pan and stir well. Bring to a boil, then reduce heat to low and simmer 5 minutes.

3. In a 2-quart saucepan over high heat, add water to fill pot ¾ full. Once water begins to boil, add pasta and salt. Cook, stirring occasionally, until pasta is al dente, about 10 minutes. Drain well and return to pot.

4. Pour prepared sauce over cooked pasta and toss to coat. Transfer to a serving plate and garnish with Parmesan and basil. Serve immediately.

Reheating Pasta
To reheat short and long pasta in sauce for your second meal, you can use your microwave, heating the pasta on high for 1 minute, then stirring gently, then heating in 45-second bursts until hot and steamy. To reheat on the stove, place in a pot and heat on medium-low until hot and steamy.

PER SERVING

Calories: 356   Fiber: 6g

Fat: 8g   Carbohydrates: 56g

Protein: 14g   Sugar: 7g

Sodium: 581mg

EGG NOODLE STIR-FRY

PREP TIME: 10 MINUTES | COOK TIME: 7 MINUTES | SERVES 1

 This savory stir-fry calls for dried lo mein noodles, but if you can find fresh lo mein noodles, feel free to use them here—just reduce the initial cooking time to 2 minutes. If you can't find either of these, you can use spaghetti cooked for 8 minutes then used as directed in the recipe.

INGREDIENTS

2 ounces dried lo mein noodles

¼ teaspoon sea salt

2 teaspoons vegetable oil, divided

½ cup frozen stir-fry vegetables

¼ cup sliced green onion, green part only, divided

2 teaspoons oyster sauce

1 teaspoon toasted sesame oil

1 teaspoon light soy sauce

1 teaspoon water

¼ teaspoon granulated sugar

¼ teaspoon sesame seeds

1. In a 2-quart saucepan over high heat, add water to fill pot ¾ full. Once water begins to boil, add lo mein noodles and salt. Cook, stirring occasionally, until tender, about 4 minutes. Rinse with cold running water to cool noodles, then toss with 1 teaspoon vegetable oil. Set aside.

2. In an 8" skillet over medium heat, add remaining 1 teaspoon vegetable oil. Once hot, add stir-fry vegetables and 3 tablespoons green onion and cook until heated through, about 3 minutes.

3. While vegetables cook, prepare sauce. In a small bowl, combine oyster sauce, sesame oil, soy sauce, water, and sugar. Set aside.

4. Once vegetables are cooked, add noodles and toss to combine. Add prepared sauce and toss well to evenly coat noodles, about 1 minute.

5. Transfer noodles to a serving dish. Garnish with remaining 1 tablespoon green onion and sesame seeds. Serve hot.

PER SERVING

Calories: 379   Fiber: 4g
Fat: 15g   Carbohydrates: 50g
Protein: 10g   Sugar: 3g
Sodium: 817mg

CREAMY SMOKED SALMON PASTA

PREP TIME: 5 MINUTES | COOK TIME: 12 MINUTES | SERVES 1

 This refreshing yet rich pasta dish makes a lovely lunch or dinner any time of year. Looking for another recipe with smoked salmon to add to your meal plan? It is also found in the Loaded Avocado Toast with Smoked Salmon (Chapter 3)!

INGREDIENTS

½ teaspoon sea salt, divided

2 ounces dried fettuccine pasta

2 teaspoons salted butter

1 clove garlic, peeled

1 teaspoon freeze-dried dill

1 teaspoon freeze-dried chives

1 teaspoon fresh lemon zest

3 tablespoons dry white wine

2 tablespoons heavy whipping cream

3 ounces smoked salmon, chopped

¼ teaspoon freshly cracked black pepper

1. In a 2-quart saucepan over high heat, add water to fill pot ¾ full. Once water begins to boil, add ¼ teaspoon salt and pasta. Cook, stirring occasionally, until pasta is al dente, about 10 minutes. Drain well and set aside.

2. In an 8" skillet over medium heat, add butter. Once melted and foaming, add garlic and cook 30 seconds. Add dill, chives, and lemon zest and cook 30 seconds, then add wine and stir well.

3. Cook garlic mixture until wine is reduced by ½, about 1 minute, then add cream and stir well. Add pasta and toss to coat in sauce, then add in salmon and toss well.

4. Transfer pasta to a serving plate and garnish with remaining ¼ teaspoon salt and pepper. Serve immediately.

PER SERVING

Calories: 513   Fiber: 3g
Fat: 22g   Carbohydrates: 47g
Protein: 25g   Sugar: 2g
Sodium: 1,218mg

GNOCCHI WITH BROWN BUTTER AND SAGE

PREP TIME: 5 MINUTES | COOK TIME: 8 MINUTES | SERVES 1

 Sage and brown butter give this dish a savory, nutty flavor, and this combination works with most types of pasta. The gnocchi here can also be used for Gnocchi with Creamy Mushroom Sauce (in this chapter) on your meal plan.

INGREDIENTS

¼ teaspoon sea salt

1 cup dried potato gnocchi

2 tablespoons salted butter

½ clove garlic, peeled and grated

⅛ teaspoon dried sage

¼ teaspoon freshly cracked black pepper

1 tablespoon grated Parmesan cheese

1. In a 2-quart saucepan over high heat, add water to fill pot ¾ full. Once water begins to boil, add salt and gnocchi. Cook, stirring occasionally, until gnocchi are floating, about 3 minutes. Reserve ¼ cup cooking water. Drain well and set aside.

2. In an 8" skillet over medium heat, add butter. Allow to melt and foam, then reduce heat to medium-low and cook, stirring often, until butter solids start to toast and become golden brown, 3–4 minutes.

3. Once butter is brown, add garlic and sage and cook 1 minute, then add gnocchi and toss to coat in sauce. If gnocchi seem dry, add reserved cooking water 1 tablespoon at a time until gnocchi are lightly but evenly coated. Add pepper and toss well, then transfer to a serving plate and garnish with Parmesan. Serve immediately.

Freezing Gnocchi
Leftover packaged gnocchi can be frozen for up to 3 months. Freeze in individual servings to make cooking easier. Do not thaw before cooking; just add frozen gnocchi to boiling salted water and add an extra 1–2 minutes to the cooking time.

PER SERVING

Calories: 467 Fiber: 3g

Fat: 23g Carbohydrates: 57g

Protein: 7g Sugar: 1g

Sodium: 931mg

PASTA BOLOGNESE

PREP TIME: 10 MINUTES | COOK TIME: 1 HOUR 24 MINUTES | SERVES 2

 This cook once, eat twice Bolognese makes two portions of sauce—one to be used right away and a second to be used with fresh cooked pasta later in the week. You can also freeze the extra sauce and use it in next week's meal plan.

INGREDIENTS

1 tablespoon olive oil

½ yellow onion, peeled and finely chopped

½ medium carrot, peeled and finely chopped

½ celery stalk, trimmed and finely chopped

2 tablespoons tomato paste

¼ pound 90/10 ground beef

¼ pound ground pork

½ cup dry red wine

1 cup plus 4 tablespoons low-sodium beef broth, divided

¼ cup whole milk

1 dried bay leaf

4 ounces dried penne pasta, divided

½ teaspoon sea salt, divided

¼ cup grated Parmesan cheese, divided

PER SERVING

Calories: 579   Fiber: 5g

Fat: 17g   Carbohydrates: 58g

Protein: 38g   Sugar: 8g

Sodium: 1,087mg

1. In an 8" nonstick skillet with a lid, add oil over medium heat. Once hot, add onion, carrot, and celery and cook until very tender, about 8 minutes. Add tomato paste and cook until tomato paste is darker in color and very thick, about 6 minutes.

2. Add beef and pork to skillet. Brown meats, crumbling well, about 5 minutes. Stir in wine and scrape bottom of pan to release any brown bits. Reduce heat to medium-low and reduce wine until almost entirely evaporated, 8–10 minutes.

3. Add 1 cup broth and milk to skillet and stir well, then add bay leaf. Bring mixture to barely a simmer, then cover pan, reduce heat to low, and cook 45 minutes, stirring occasionally.

4. When sauce is done simmering, remove lid and discard bay leaf. Mixture should resemble thick chili. If mixture seems too dry, add 2–4 tablespoons broth to loosen. Remove from heat and cover to keep warm.

5. In a 2-quart saucepan over high heat, add water to fill pot ¾ full. Once water begins to boil, add 2 ounces pasta and ¼ teaspoon salt. Cook, stirring occasionally, until pasta is al dente, about 10 minutes. Drain well and return to pot. Add ½ of sauce mixture and toss to coat.

6. Transfer pasta to a serving plate and top with 2 tablespoons Parmesan. Serve immediately or refrigerate reserved sauce and remaining 2 tablespoons Parmesan in an airtight container.

CHICKEN TETRAZZINI

PREP TIME: 20 MINUTES | COOK TIME: 44 MINUTES | SERVES 1

 This creamy baked pasta uses a béchamel sauce enhanced with a bit of chicken broth for flavor. You can prepare this dish up to the point of baking, cover, and refrigerate it for up to 3 days. When ready, just bake as directed, adding 3–5 extra minutes.

INGREDIENTS

1 tablespoon salted butter

½ cup sliced button mushrooms

¼ cup chopped yellow onion

1 clove garlic, peeled and minced

¼ teaspoon Italian seasoning

¼ cup dry white wine

1 tablespoon all-purpose flour

⅓ cup whole milk

¼ cup low-sodium chicken broth

⅛ teaspoon ground nutmeg

½ cup shredded cooked chicken breast

2 ounces dried linguine pasta

¾ teaspoon sea salt, divided

¼ teaspoon freshly cracked black pepper

2 tablespoons grated Parmesan cheese

PER SERVING

Calories: 607
Fat: 19g
Protein: 38g
Sodium: 967mg

Fiber: 4g
Carbohydrates: 61g
Sugar: 8g

1. Preheat oven to 350°F and spray a 1-quart baking dish with nonstick cooking spray.

2. In an 8" skillet over medium heat, add butter. Once melted, swirl to coat bottom of pan evenly, then add mushrooms. Cook, stirring occasionally, until mushrooms are lightly golden brown, about 5 minutes. Add onion and cook 2 minutes, then add garlic and Italian seasoning and cook 30 seconds or until fragrant.

3. Add wine to skillet and cook, scraping any bits off bottom of pan, until fully evaporated, about 3 minutes. Sprinkle flour over top, stir well, and cook 1 minute.

4. Reduce heat to medium-low and stir in milk and broth. Cook, stirring constantly, until sauce thickly coats the back of a spoon, about 2 minutes. Turn off heat and stir in nutmeg, then fold in chicken. Set aside.

5. In a 2-quart saucepan over high heat, add water to fill pot ¾ full. Once water begins to boil, add pasta and ½ teaspoon salt. Cook, stirring occasionally, until pasta is al dente, about 10 minutes. Reserve ¼ cup pasta water, then drain well.

6. Add remaining ¼ teaspoon salt, pepper, reserved pasta water, and pasta to skillet with sauce and toss to combine. Transfer to prepared dish and sprinkle with Parmesan. Bake 20 minutes or until Parmesan is golden brown on top. Cool 5 minutes before serving.

CAJUN CHICKEN PASTA

PREP TIME: 10 MINUTES | COOK TIME: 17 MINUTES | SERVES 1

 This pasta dish is creamy, spicy, and loaded with protein to help keep you full! It is also a great recipe to use up leftover smoked sausage, shredded chicken, and fresh tomatoes from other recipes in your plan.

INGREDIENTS

2 ounces dried rotini pasta

½ teaspoon sea salt

1 tablespoon unsalted butter

¼ cup chopped yellow onion

¼ cup chopped green bell pepper

2 tablespoons chopped celery

¼ cup diced Roma tomato

½ teaspoon Cajun seasoning

1 tablespoon all-purpose flour

½ cup low-sodium chicken broth

2 tablespoons heavy whipping cream

⅓ cup shredded cooked chicken breast

⅓ cup sliced smoked sausage

1. In a 2-quart saucepan over high heat, add water to fill pot ¾ full. Once water begins to boil, add pasta and salt. Cook, stirring occasionally, until pasta is al dente, about 10 minutes. Drain well and set aside.

2. Return pot to medium heat and add butter. Once melted, swirl to coat bottom of pan, then add onion, bell pepper, and celery. Cook, stirring often, until vegetables are softened, about 3 minutes. Add tomato and Cajun seasoning. Cook until Cajun seasoning is fragrant, about 30 seconds.

3. Sprinkle flour evenly over vegetables and mix well. Cook, stirring constantly, 1 minute. Slowly stir in broth, mixing well to make sure there are no lumps. Cook, stirring constantly, until sauce comes to a simmer and thickens, 1–2 minutes.

4. Reduce heat to low and stir in cream, chicken, and sausage. Add pasta and fold to combine. Serve hot.

PER SERVING

Calories: 673   Fiber: 5g

Fat: 35g   Carbohydrates: 53g

Protein: 31g   Sugar: 6g

Sodium: 827mg

CACIO E PEPE

PREP TIME: 5 MINUTES | COOK TIME: 11 MINUTES | SERVES 1

 Translating from Italian to "cheese and pepper," this simple dish is the ultimate in comfort in a hurry. For the best texture and flavor, use freshly grated Parmesan. Wedges of fresh Parmesan keep, wrapped in parchment and refrigerated, for up to 2 weeks.

INGREDIENTS

2 ounces dried spaghetti pasta

½ teaspoon sea salt

2 tablespoons unsalted butter

½ teaspoon freshly cracked black pepper

½ cup freshly grated Parmesan cheese

1. In a 2-quart saucepan over high heat, add water to fill pot ¾ full. Once water begins to boil, add pasta and salt. Cook, stirring occasionally, until pasta is just al dente, about 9 minutes. Reserve ⅓ cup pasta water, then drain well.

2. Return pot to medium heat and add butter. Once melted, add pepper and cook 30 seconds, then slowly stir in ¼ cup reserved pasta water.

3. Add pasta to pot and toss well, then reduce heat to low and add Parmesan. Toss until evenly combined and sauce is thick, about 1 minute. If mixture is too dry, add additional pasta water and toss well. Serve immediately.

PER SERVING

Calories: 634   Fiber: 3g

Fat: 34g   Carbohydrates: 51g

Protein: 23g   Sugar: 1g

Sodium: 1,088mg

CREAMY PESTO RAVIOLI

PREP TIME: 5 MINUTES | COOK TIME: 6 MINUTES | SERVES 1

 Frozen ravioli are an awesome ingredient to keep on hand for easy meal planning. This dish also uses baby spinach, which is found in the Seven Layer Salad in Chapter 5 and the Spinach and Cheddar Twice-Baked Potato in Chapter 7.

INGREDIENTS

2 ounces frozen large cheese ravioli

½ teaspoon sea salt

1 teaspoon olive oil

2 tablespoons finely chopped yellow onion

1 cup lightly packed fresh baby spinach

2 tablespoons basil pesto

1 tablespoon heavy whipping cream

2 tablespoons grated Parmesan cheese

⅛ teaspoon crushed red pepper flakes

1. In a 2-quart saucepan over high heat, add water to fill pot ¾ full. Once water begins to boil, add ravioli and salt. Cook, stirring occasionally, until ravioli start to float, about 4 minutes. Drain well and set aside.

2. Return pot to medium heat and add oil. Once hot, add onion and cook 1 minute, then add spinach and cook, stirring constantly, until wilted, about 1 minute.

3. Add pesto to pot and mix well, then stir in cream and ravioli and turn to coat ravioli evenly. Transfer to a serving plate and top with Parmesan and red pepper flakes. Serve immediately.

Homemade Pesto Sauce

Pesto is a snap to make at home! For ⅓ cup of pesto, just add 1 cup basil leaves, ¼ cup extra-virgin olive oil, 3 tablespoons freshly grated Parmesan cheese, 2 tablespoons pine nuts, ½ clove garlic (peeled), and ⅛ teaspoon sea salt to a food processor and purée until smooth. Store in an airtight container for up to 2 weeks.

PER SERVING

Calories: 365   Fiber: 2g

Fat: 26g   Carbohydrates: 23g

Protein: 10g   Sugar: 3g

Sodium: 718mg

SESAME GARLIC SOBA NOODLES

PREP TIME: 10 MINUTES | COOK TIME: 4 MINUTES | SERVES 1

 This dish can be enjoyed right away or served chilled for a meal on the go. To add an extra kick, feel free to toss in ½ teaspoon of the chili crisp used in the Soba Noodles with Peanut Sauce in this chapter.

INGREDIENTS

1 clove garlic, peeled and minced

2 teaspoons light soy sauce

1 teaspoon hot chili sauce

1 teaspoon white miso paste

1 teaspoon toasted sesame oil

½ teaspoon rice wine vinegar

2 ounces dried soba noodles

½ teaspoon sea salt

1 large medium-boiled egg, halved lengthwise

2 tablespoons diced English cucumber

2 tablespoons sliced green onion, green part only

¼ teaspoon toasted sesame seeds

1. In a medium bowl, add garlic, soy sauce, chili sauce, miso paste, sesame oil, and vinegar. Whisk well. Set aside.

2. In a 2-quart saucepan over high heat, add water to fill pot ¾ full. Once water begins to boil, add soba noodles and salt. Cook, stirring occasionally, until noodles are tender, about 4 minutes. Drain well.

3. Transfer noodles to bowl with sauce and toss to coat. Transfer to a serving plate and top with egg, cucumber, and green onion. Sprinkle with sesame seeds. Serve immediately.

PER SERVING

Calories: 260   Fiber: 1g

Fat: 9g   Carbohydrates: 30g

Protein: 14g   Sugar: 3g

Sodium: 1,126mg

SOBA NOODLES WITH PEANUT SAUCE

PREP TIME: 10 MINUTES | COOK TIME: 8 MINUTES | SERVES 1

 The indulgent peanut butter sauce for these noodles would also make a wonderful dressing for a chopped Asian salad. The coleslaw mix from this recipe is also used in the Pork Egg Roll in a Bowl (Chapter 9), so add it to the same week's meal plan!

INGREDIENTS

1 tablespoon creamy peanut butter

2 teaspoons light soy sauce

1 teaspoon chili crisp, such as Laoganma

1 teaspoon honey

½ teaspoon toasted sesame oil

½ teaspoon rice wine vinegar

2 ounces dried soba noodles

½ teaspoon sea salt

2 teaspoons vegetable oil

¼ large red bell pepper, seeded and thinly sliced

¼ cup thinly sliced yellow onion

1 cup bagged coleslaw mix

½ clove garlic, peeled and minced

2 tablespoons sliced green onion, green part only

1. In a small bowl, combine peanut butter, soy sauce, chili crisp, honey, sesame oil, and vinegar. Set aside.

2. In a 2-quart saucepan over high heat, add water to fill pot ¾ full. Once water begins to boil, add soba noodles and salt. Cook, stirring occasionally, until tender, about 4 minutes. Drain well and set aside.

3. Return pot to medium heat and add vegetable oil. Once hot, add bell pepper and onion. Cook until just tender, about 2 minutes. Add coleslaw mix and garlic and cook, stirring often, until coleslaw is wilted and soft, about 2 minutes.

4. Add noodles and prepared sauce to pot. Toss to evenly combine sauce, noodles, and vegetables. Transfer to a serving plate and garnish with green onion. Serve hot.

Easy Coleslaw

You can whip up two side servings of coleslaw when preparing this meal by mixing 3 tablespoons mayonnaise, 2 tablespoons diced yellow onion, 1 tablespoon granulated sugar, 2 teaspoons white vinegar, ¼ teaspoon freshly cracked black pepper, and ⅛ teaspoon sea salt, then folding in 2 cups of bagged coleslaw mix. Cover and refrigerate at least 2 hours, up to 5 days.

PER SERVING

Calories: 340	Fiber: 5g
Fat: 14g	Carbohydrates: 47g
Protein: 13g	Sugar: 14g
Sodium: 799mg	

PASTA PRIMAVERA

PREP TIME: 10 MINUTES | COOK TIME: 19 MINUTES | SERVES 1

 Looking for a recipe to use up vegetable scraps from your week of meal planning? Look no further! Feel free to add or substitute vegetables such as bell peppers, mushrooms, spinach, cabbage, and onions in this recipe.

INGREDIENTS

2 ounces dried penne pasta

¾ teaspoon sea salt, divided

1 tablespoon olive oil

½ cup fresh broccoli florets, chopped

¼ cup chopped zucchini

¼ cup chopped yellow squash

¼ cup chopped Roma tomato

1 clove garlic, peeled and minced

2 tablespoons dry white wine

¼ teaspoon freshly cracked black pepper

1 fresh basil leaf, chopped

1. In a 2-quart saucepan over high heat, add water to fill pot ¾ full. Once water begins to boil, add pasta and ½ teaspoon salt. Cook, stirring occasionally, until pasta is just al dente, about 10 minutes. Drain and set aside.

2. Return pot to medium heat and add oil. Once hot, add broccoli, zucchini, and squash and cook until just tender, about 5 minutes. Add tomato and cook until soft and tender, about 2 minutes. Add garlic and cook until fragrant, about 1 minute.

3. Add wine, remaining ¼ teaspoon salt, and pepper to pot and toss to combine, then let wine reduce by half, about 1 minute.

4. Transfer pasta to a serving plate. Pour vegetables and sauce over top. Garnish with basil. Enjoy immediately.

PER SERVING

Calories: 383   Fiber: 5g
Fat: 14g   Carbohydrates: 50g
Protein: 11g   Sugar: 4g
Sodium: 592mg

GARLIC BUTTER SHRIMP PASTA

PREP TIME: 5 MINUTES | COOK TIME: 14 MINUTES | SERVES 1

 Fast, filling, and fancy, this buttery shrimp pasta is a great recipe to add to your week's meal plan for busy days or when you have extra shrimp in the freezer that you want to use up. Add a slice of crusty French bread on the side to soak up the sauce.

INGREDIENTS

2 ounces dried fettuccine pasta

½ teaspoon sea salt

2 tablespoons salted butter

1 clove garlic, peeled and roughly chopped

3 ounces frozen large shrimp, peeled and deveined

2 teaspoons fresh lemon juice

1 tablespoon chopped fresh parsley

¼ teaspoon freshly cracked black pepper

1. In a 2-quart saucepan over high heat, add water to fill pot ¾ full. Once water begins to boil, add pasta and salt. Cook, stirring occasionally, until pasta is just al dente, about 10 minutes. Reserve ¼ cup pasta water. Drain well and set aside.

2. Return pot to medium heat and add butter. Once melted and foaming, add garlic and cook 1 minute or until very fragrant. Add shrimp and cook, stirring often, until shrimp are curled into C shapes and are opaque, about 3 minutes.

3. Add 1 tablespoon pasta water and lemon juice to shrimp and stir well, then add pasta and toss to coat in butter and garlic. Add more pasta water 1 tablespoon at a time until pasta is evenly coated. Add parsley and pepper and toss to coat.

4. Transfer pasta to a plate and serve immediately.

Thawing Frozen Shrimp
When you are ready to enjoy your frozen shrimp, remove the amount you need from the package to a plastic bag in a medium bowl. Add room temperature water to bowl and let stand 20 minutes or until thawed. Cook right away.

PER SERVING

Calories: 490   Fiber: 3g
Fat: 23g   Carbohydrates: 46g
Protein: 20g   Sugar: 1g
Sodium: 848mg

GNOCCHI WITH CREAMY MUSHROOM SAUCE

PREP TIME: 10 MINUTES | COOK TIME: 22 MINUTES | SERVES 1

 Switch up your gnocchi game by pan-frying them until crisp, then simmering them in sauce until tender. This method adds a richer flavor while keeping the gnocchi fluffy.

INGREDIENTS

1 tablespoon vegetable oil

4 ounces dried potato gnocchi

1 tablespoon salted butter

¼ cup finely chopped yellow onion

1 clove garlic, peeled and minced

½ cup sliced button mushrooms

½ cup lightly packed fresh baby spinach, roughly chopped

½ cup low-sodium chicken broth

2 tablespoons heavy whipping cream

⅛ teaspoon ground nutmeg

2 tablespoons grated Parmesan cheese

¼ teaspoon freshly cracked black pepper

1. In an 8" skillet over medium-high heat, add oil. Once hot, swirl pan to coat bottom, then add gnocchi. Cook until browned on first side, 2–3 minutes, then stir pan and continue to cook, flipping gnocchi every 2 minutes, until golden brown and crisp around edges, 5–8 minutes.

2. Add butter to skillet and melt, then add onion and cook 1 minute. Add garlic and cook 30 seconds. Add mushrooms and spinach and cook, stirring often, until mushrooms are tender and spinach is wilted, about 3 minutes.

3. Stir in broth, scraping bottom of pan to release any brown bits. Bring to a simmer and cook 1 minute. Reduce heat to medium-low and stir in cream and nutmeg and simmer until liquid is reduced by ⅔, about 5 minutes. Do not boil.

4. Once sauce is reduced, stir in Parmesan and pepper. Transfer to a plate and enjoy hot.

PER SERVING

Calories: 567
Fat: 38g
Protein: 10g
Sodium: 791mg

Fiber: 4g
Carbohydrates: 47g
Sugar: 4g

VEGETARIAN MAIN DISHES

Having a balanced diet that includes plenty of vegetables and whole grains is easier when you practice weekly meal planning. You have the option to build meals with foods that work for your preferences and needs, and you do not have to worry about sacrificing flavor or satisfaction. From lighter meals that will not weigh you down to hearty fare that will fill you up, there is a vegetarian meal sure to satisfy any mood, season, or craving. No matter the reason, enjoying more vegetarian and plant-based meals is a good idea!

This chapter has a variety of vegetarian main meals that are perfect for lunches and dinners and can be enjoyed alone or with your favorite side dishes. If you want an easy all-in-one meal for your plan, try the Fall Root Vegetable Stew or the Vegetable Lover's Pizza. If you want to pair your main dish with a side, why not add the Chickpea Masala with the Saffron Rice (Chapter 5), or the Black Bean Tacos with Corn and Tomato Relish with the Vegetarian Charro Beans (Chapter 5)? Meal planning vegetarian-based dishes means you can look forward to feel-good and good-for-you options all week! Four recipes are two servings, so you can enjoy them again without the prep or active cook time.

BLACK BEAN TACOS WITH CORN AND TOMATO RELISH

PREP TIME: 15 MINUTES | COOK TIME: 4 MINUTES | SERVES 1

 Warm seasoned beans, fresh corn and tomato relish, and smooth sour cream make this a meal you will want to add to your meal plan again and again. The leftover black beans can be used in the Quick Black Bean Soup (Chapter 5).

INGREDIENTS

¼ cup diced Roma tomato

¼ cup frozen corn kernels, thawed

2 tablespoons finely chopped yellow onion, divided

1 teaspoon fresh lime juice

2 teaspoons vegetable oil, divided

½ teaspoon ground cumin, divided

½ teaspoon chili powder, divided

½ cup drained and rinsed canned black beans

1 tablespoon chopped fresh cilantro

½ clove garlic, peeled and minced

2 (6") yellow corn tortillas

2 tablespoons sour cream

PER SERVING

Calories: 397   Fiber: 14g

Fat: 15g   Carbohydrates: 55g

Protein: 13g   Sugar: 4g

Sodium: 346mg

1. In a small bowl, add tomato, corn, 1 tablespoon onion, lime juice, ½ teaspoon oil, ¼ teaspoon cumin, and ¼ teaspoon chili powder. Mix well and set aside.

2. In an 8" skillet over medium heat, add remaining 1½ teaspoons oil. Once hot, swirl to coat bottom of skillet, then add remaining 1 tablespoon onion. Cook until just translucent, about 1 minute. Add remaining ¼ teaspoon each cumin and chili powder and cook 30 seconds.

3. Add beans, cilantro, and garlic to skillet and cook, stirring frequently, until beans are hot and garlic is fragrant, about 2 minutes. Remove from heat.

4. Wrap tortillas in a damp paper towel and heat in microwave 20 seconds on high, then flip and heat 10 seconds on high.

5. To serve, divide bean mixture between tortillas, top with equal amounts sour cream, and divide corn and tomato relish over top. Serve immediately.

Make It a Tostada

You can easily turn this dish into a tostada! Heat the oven to 375°F and line a ½ sheet pan with baking parchment. Lay tortillas on prepared sheet pan and bake 8 minutes, then flip and bake 8–10 minutes or until tortillas are crisp. Cool 3 minutes, then top with beans, sour cream, and relish.

VEGETABLE SUMMER ROLLS

PREP TIME: 15 MINUTES | COOK TIME: 3 MINUTES | SERVES 1

 These vegetable rolls are best when enjoyed the day they are made so the wrapper stays firm and chewy, but you can make them up to 1 day ahead. Just wrap each roll in plastic wrap, place in an airtight container, and keep chilled until you're ready to enjoy.

INGREDIENTS

1 tablespoon creamy peanut butter

1 teaspoon chili crisp, such as Laoganma

½ teaspoon toasted sesame oil

½ teaspoon fresh lime juice

¼ teaspoon packed light brown sugar

1 ounce thin rice noodles

1 cup boiling water

2 large iceberg lettuce leaves

¼ cup shredded purple cabbage

¼ cup julienned English cucumber

¼ cup julienned carrot

½ medium avocado, pitted, peeled, and sliced

2 tablespoons chopped fresh cilantro

1 teaspoon chopped fresh mint

2 (8½") rice paper wrappers

1. In a small bowl, combine peanut butter, chili crisp, sesame oil, lime juice, and sugar. Set aside.

2. Place rice noodles in a medium bowl. Pour boiling water over noodles. Let stand 3 minutes, then drain well and rise in cool water.

3. On a work surface, lay down lettuce leaves. Divide cabbage, cucumber, carrot, avocado, cilantro, and mint evenly and place on leaves. Divide noodles over top of vegetables. Set aside.

4. Fill a shallow dish with cool water. Dip one rice paper wrapper into water for 2 seconds, then lay on a work surface. Place one filled lettuce leaf onto center of paper. Fold sides of paper over filling, then pull edge of wrapper closest to you over center and roll forward to make a roll. Repeat with second wrapper and filling. Enjoy immediately with dipping sauce.

Spring Roll Addition

For extra protein, you can add to each roll a 1-ounce strip of firm tofu that has been drained well to remove excess water. You can also use baked tofu that is available in the refrigerated produce or vegetarian section.

PER SERVING

Calories: 381   Fiber: 8g

Fat: 23g   Carbohydrates: 39g

Protein: 8g   Sugar: 8g

Sodium: 164mg

VEGETABLE AND LENTIL STEW

PREP TIME: 10 MINUTES | COOK TIME: 38 MINUTES | SERVES 2

 The frozen root vegetable blend makes this cook once, eat twice stew fast to prepare. If frozen root vegetable blend is not available, you can use a mix of chopped carrot, sweet potato, turnip, and beet that equals 1 cup. Freeze the rest for future meal plans!

INGREDIENTS

2 tablespoons vegetable oil

½ cup chopped yellow onion

½ cup chopped celery

1 clove garlic, peeled and minced

½ teaspoon smoked paprika

¼ teaspoon dried thyme

1 (6-ounce) unpeeled russet potato, chopped

½ cup dried green lentils, rinsed and drained

2 cups low-sodium vegetable broth

1 dried bay leaf

1 cup frozen mixed root vegetables

½ teaspoon fresh lemon juice

1. In a 2-quart pot with a lid over medium heat, add oil. Once hot, add onion and celery and cook until tender, about 5 minutes. Add garlic, paprika, and thyme and cook until fragrant, about 30 seconds.

2. Add potato and lentils to pot and stir to combine. Stir in broth and bay leaf. Bring mixture to a boil over medium heat, then reduce heat to medium-low, cover pot, and simmer 20 minutes.

3. Add root vegetable blend, stir well, return lid to pot, and simmer 12 minutes or until lentils are tender.

4. Remove lid and discard bay leaf. Stir in lemon juice, then remove from heat and let cool 3 minutes before serving hot.

PER SERVING

Calories: 440   Fiber: 11g

Fat: 14g   Carbohydrates: 63mg

Protein: 16g   Sugar: 10g

Sodium: 198mg

CHICKPEA MASALA

PREP TIME: 10 MINUTES | COOK TIME: 15 MINUTES | SERVES 2

 This dish is a vegetarian version of chicken tikka masala, with roasted chickpeas used in place of the roasted chicken. It makes excellent leftovers since the flavor improves with time, so enjoy this recipe for a lunch and dinner in your meal plan!

INGREDIENTS

1 (15-ounce) can chickpeas, drained and rinsed

2 tablespoons vegetable oil, divided

½ cup chopped yellow onion

1 clove garlic, peeled and minced

½ teaspoon garam masala

¼ teaspoon ground cumin

¼ teaspoon ground coriander

¼ teaspoon ground ginger

¼ teaspoon sea salt

¼ teaspoon packed light brown sugar

½ cup canned crushed tomatoes, undrained

¼ cup water

¼ cup heavy whipping cream

1 tablespoon chopped fresh cilantro

1. Preheat oven to 400°F and line a ½ sheet pan with baking parchment.

2. Place chickpeas on prepared sheet pan. Drizzle with 1 tablespoon oil and toss to coat. Bake 15 minutes, stirring every 5 minutes.

3. While chickpeas roast, prepare sauce. In a 2-quart saucepan over medium heat, add remaining 1 tablespoon oil. Once hot, swirl to coat bottom of pot and add onion. Cook, stirring often, until very tender, about 5 minutes. Add garlic, garam masala, cumin, coriander, ginger, salt, and sugar and mix well. Cook until spices are very fragrant, about 1 minute.

4. Stir in tomato, scraping bottom of pot to release any brown bits. Add water and mix well. Bring mixture to a boil, then reduce heat to medium-low and simmer until reduced by ⅓, about 5 minutes.

5. Stir in chickpeas and cream. Transfer to a serving bowl and garnish with cilantro. Enjoy hot.

PER SERVING

Calories: 447   Fiber: 10g
Fat: 26g   Carbohydrates: 40g
Protein: 11g   Sugar: 10g
Sodium: 607mg

STACKED BLACK BEAN AND CHEESE ENCHILADAS

PREP TIME: 10 MINUTES | COOK TIME: 27 MINUTES | SERVES 1

 Enchiladas make a hearty meal, and this dish is a great place to use up black beans and tomatoes left over from other recipes on your meal plan. If you have corn in the freezer, you can add 2 tablespoons of it to the filling.

INGREDIENTS

2 teaspoons vegetable oil

½ clove garlic, peeled and minced

¼ teaspoon ground cumin

⅛ teaspoon chili powder

½ cup drained and rinsed canned black beans

2 tablespoons diced Roma tomato

½ teaspoon fresh lime juice

¼ cup red enchilada sauce

2 (6") yellow corn tortillas

½ cup shredded sharp Cheddar cheese

2 tablespoons chopped yellow onion

1. Preheat oven to 375°F and spray a 6" baking dish with nonstick cooking spray.

2. In an 8" skillet over medium heat, add oil. Once hot, swirl to coat bottom of pan. Add garlic, cumin, and chili powder and cook 30 seconds, then add beans and tomato and cook until beans are hot, about 1 minute. Remove from heat and stir in lime juice.

3. In a small dish, add enchilada sauce. Dip 1 tortilla into sauce and place into prepared dish. Top with ½ of bean mixture, ¼ cup Cheddar, and 1 tablespoon onion. Repeat with remaining ingredients. Pour any leftover sauce over top of dish.

4. Bake 20–25 minutes until cheese is melted and bubbling. Cool 5 minutes before serving. Enjoy warm.

Cilantro Lime Rice for One

Whip up a zesty side of rice for this dish: In a small pot with a lid, add ¼ cup long-grain white rice (rinsed and drained), ½ cup water, 1 tablespoon chopped fresh cilantro, 1 teaspoon vegetable oil, 1 teaspoon freshly grated lime zest, and ⅛ teaspoon sea salt. Bring to a boil over medium heat, cover, reduce heat to low, and simmer 20 minutes. Remove from heat and let stand 15 minutes. Fluff and enjoy.

PER SERVING

Calories: 564
Fat: 27g
Protein: 25g
Sodium: 1,186mg

Fiber: 13g
Carbohydrates: 51g
Sugar: 6g

SUMMER VEGETABLE FLATBREAD

PREP TIME: 20 MINUTES | COOK TIME: 20 MINUTES | SERVES 1

 Fresh vegetables and creamy ricotta make this a refreshing yet satisfying meal. While this recipe calls for summer vegetables, feel free to use your favorite seasonal vegetables for a tasty addition to your meal plan any time of year. For example, in the fall, thinly sliced carrot, chopped broccoli, and spinach would be a delicious combo!

INGREDIENTS

⅓ cup all-purpose flour, plus extra for dusting

¼ teaspoon baking powder

¼ teaspoon sea salt, divided

2 teaspoons olive oil, divided

2 tablespoons warm water

1 teaspoon vegetable oil

¼ cup whole milk ricotta cheese

¼ cup shredded mozzarella cheese

¼ cup cherry tomatoes, sliced in half

¼ cup thinly sliced red onion

¼ cup sliced zucchini

¼ cup chopped red bell pepper

¼ teaspoon Italian seasoning

¼ teaspoon freshly cracked black pepper

2 fresh basil leaves, roughly torn

PER SERVING

Calories: 477   Fiber: 3g

Fat: 25g   Carbohydrates: 43g

Protein: 18g   Sugar: 5g

Sodium: 714mg

1. Preheat oven to 400°F and line a ½ sheet pan with baking parchment.

2. In a medium bowl, add flour, baking powder, and ⅛ teaspoon salt. Whisk to combine. Add 1 teaspoon olive oil and water. Mix until a dough ball forms, adding additional water if needed a few drops at a time. Cover bowl and let rest 10 minutes.

3. Turn dough ball out onto a lightly floured surface. Roll into a ¼"-thick circle, about 8" in diameter. Cover and let rest while skillet heats.

4. Heat an 8" skillet over medium heat. Add vegetable oil and swirl to coat pan. Add flatbread and cook 2–3 minutes on one side until golden brown, then flip and cook 2 minutes or until second side is golden and flatbread is puffed.

5. Remove flatbread from skillet and transfer to prepared sheet pan. Spread ricotta on flatbread in an even layer. Sprinkle with mozzarella, then top with tomatoes, onion, zucchini, and bell pepper. Sprinkle Italian seasoning, black pepper, and remaining ⅛ teaspoon salt over top. Drizzle remaining 1 teaspoon olive oil over top and dot with torn basil.

6. Bake 15 minutes or until cheese is melted and vegetables are tender. Cool 3 minutes before enjoying.

CAULIFLOWER FRIED RICE

PREP TIME: 10 MINUTES | COOK TIME: 10 MINUTES | SERVES 1

 This version of fried rice is absolutely loaded with vegetables and is an awesome place to add other ingredients from your kitchen, like chopped leftover cubed tofu, sliced mushrooms, or frozen stir-fry vegetables. Frozen riced cauliflower is an excellent freezer staple to keep ready for weekly meal planning.

INGREDIENTS

1⅓ cups frozen riced cauliflower, thawed

1 tablespoon plus 1 teaspoon vegetable oil, divided

1 large egg, beaten

¼ cup chopped carrot

¼ cup chopped yellow onion

¼ cup frozen peas

1 clove garlic, peeled and minced

2 teaspoons light soy sauce

2 teaspoons hoisin sauce

2 tablespoons sliced green onion, green part only

1. In an 8" skillet over medium heat, add cauliflower. Cook, stirring often, until cauliflower is dry and lightly golden around edges, about 5 minutes. Transfer to a small bowl and set aside.

2. Return pan to medium heat and add 1 teaspoon oil. Once hot, swirl to coat bottom of pan. Add egg and scramble until egg is set, 45–50 seconds. Transfer to bowl with cauliflower and set aside.

3. Return pan to medium-high heat and add remaining 1 tablespoon oil. Once hot, swirl to coat bottom of pan. Add carrot and onion and cook until tender, about 2 minutes. Add peas and cook 30 seconds, then add garlic and cook until fragrant, about 30 seconds. Add cauliflower and egg to skillet and mix to combine.

4. Make a well in center of mixture and add soy sauce to well. Cook 10 seconds, then stir into rice along with hoisin sauce.

5. Transfer to a serving plate and garnish with green onion. Serve immediately.

PER SERVING

Calories: 351	Fiber: 7g
Fat: 23g	Carbohydrates: 24g
Protein: 13g	Sugar: 11g
Sodium: 911mg	

ORZO AND VEGETABLE–STUFFED PEPPER

PREP TIME: 10 MINUTES | COOK TIME: 1 HOUR 3 MINUTES | SERVES 1

 If bell peppers are on sale, add this recipe to your meal plan! It is filling but won't weight you down, and you can prepare it up until you place the bell pepper in the oven and instead refrigerate it for up to 3 days before cooking and serving.

INGREDIENTS

1½ cups low-sodium vegetable broth

¼ teaspoon sea salt

¼ cup dried orzo pasta

2 teaspoons vegetable oil

2 tablespoons chopped yellow onion

½ cup lightly packed fresh baby spinach, roughly chopped

½ clove garlic, peeled and minced

1 teaspoon tomato paste

½ teaspoon Italian seasoning

1 large red bell pepper

2 tablespoons shredded mozzarella cheese

1. Preheat oven to 400°F and spray a 6" baking dish with nonstick cooking spray.

2. In a 1-quart saucepan, add broth and salt. Heat over medium heat until boiling. Add pasta and cook until al dente, about 8 minutes. Drain and rinse with cool water to stop cooking. Set aside.

3. In an 8" skillet over medium heat, add oil. Once hot, swirl to coat bottom of pan, then add onion. Cook 30 seconds, then add spinach and cook, stirring constantly, until wilted, about 1 minute. Add garlic and cook 30 seconds, then add tomato paste and Italian seasoning and cook 1 minute.

4. Add pasta to pan and stir to mix well. Remove from heat and set aside.

5. Slice top off bell pepper and remove ribs and seeds, then cut a thin slice off bottom to help pepper remain stable in baking dish. Place pepper in prepared dish.

6. Spoon filling into pepper, cover dish with aluminum foil, and bake 35–40 minutes or until pepper is tender.

7. Remove aluminum foil and top pepper with mozzarella. Bake 10–12 minutes or until cheese is melted. Cool 3 minutes before serving.

PER SERVING

Calories: 338
Fat: 12g
Protein: 11g
Sodium: 289mg
Fiber: 6g
Carbohydrates: 45g
Sugar: 8g

SPINACH AND FETA–STUFFED MUSHROOM

PREP TIME: 10 MINUTES | COOK TIME: 25 MINUTES | SERVES 1

 This creamy, cheesy stuffed mushroom gets a flavor boost from the tangy feta. The Mediterranean Pasta Salad (Chapter 5) also uses feta cheese, so consider that for your meal plan if you are also making this main dish!

INGREDIENTS

½ cup water

¼ teaspoon sea salt

2 tablespoons dried orzo pasta

1 large portobello mushroom cap, gills removed

2 teaspoons vegetable oil, divided

2 tablespoons minced yellow onion

1 cup lightly packed fresh baby spinach, chopped

½ clove garlic, peeled and minced

⅛ teaspoon crushed red pepper flakes

2 tablespoons crumbled feta cheese

1 tablespoon cream cheese, at room temperature

PER SERVING

Calories: 289   Fiber: 3g
Fat: 18g   Carbohydrates: 24g
Protein: 9g   Sugar: 5g
Sodium: 292mg

1. Preheat broiler to 500°F and line a ¼ sheet pan with aluminum foil lightly sprayed with nonstick cooking spray.

2. In a 1-quart saucepan, add water and salt. Heat over medium heat until boiling. Add pasta and cook until al dente, about 8 minutes. Drain and rinse with cool water to stop cooking. Set aside.

3. Lightly brush mushroom with ½ teaspoon oil and place on prepared sheet pan. Broil 3–4 minutes per side until mushroom is tender. Remove from oven and set aside.

4. In an 8" skillet over medium heat, add remaining 1½ teaspoons oil and swirl to coat bottom of pan. Add onion and cook until tender, about 2 minutes. Add spinach and cook until completely wilted, about 2 minutes. Add garlic and red pepper flakes and cook until mixture is fragrant, about 1 minute.

5. Remove pan from heat and stir in pasta, feta, and cream cheese. Mix until cream cheese is melted, about 30 seconds.

6. Drain any liquids off sheet pan and place mushroom cap top-side down. Spoon filling into mushroom cap and broil 2–3 minutes until filling is golden brown on top. Serve hot.

SPINACH AND CHEDDAR TWICE-BAKED POTATO

PREP TIME: 15 MINUTES | COOK TIME: 1 HOUR 38 MINUTES | SERVES 1

 This all-in-one vegetarian main dish will hit the spot when you are craving a baked potato or when the weather is getting cooler. You can make this potato up to the point of the second bake, cover, and refrigerate it for up to 3 days, then bake 35–40 minutes at 350°F until top of mushroom is golden brown. Cool 5 minutes before serving.

INGREDIENTS

1 (8-ounce) russet potato, scrubbed and dried

¼ teaspoon olive oil

2 teaspoons vegetable oil

½ clove garlic, peeled and minced

2 cups lightly packed fresh baby spinach, roughly chopped

3 tablespoons sliced green onion, green part only, divided

2 tablespoons cream cheese, at room temperature

1 tablespoon salted butter

1 tablespoon heavy whipping cream

¼ teaspoon sea salt

¼ teaspoon freshly cracked black pepper

⅓ cup shredded sharp Cheddar cheese, divided

¼ teaspoon smoked paprika

PER SERVING

Calories: 724   Fiber: 9g
Fat: 37g   Carbohydrates: 71g
Protein: 21g   Sugar: 5g
Sodium: 923mg

1. Preheat oven to 400°F.

2. With a paring knife, poke six holes into potato, three on each side. Rub skin with olive oil.

3. Place potato directly on oven rack and bake 60–70 minutes until a paring knife slips easily in and out of potato flesh. Remove potato from oven and let cool 15 minutes.

4. Reduce oven to 350°F.

5. In an 8" skillet over medium heat, add vegetable oil. Once hot, swirl to coat bottom of pan, then add garlic. Cook 20 seconds, then add spinach and 2 tablespoons green onion. Cook, stirring constantly, until spinach is wilted and very hot, about 2 minutes. Remove from heat and set aside.

6. Once potato has cooled, slice top ⅛ of potato off. Scoop potato flesh, leaving about ¼" of flesh in skin, into a small bowl. Add cream cheese, butter, cream, salt, and pepper. Mix, stirring until mixture is well combined. Fold in ¼ cup Cheddar and spinach mixture.

7. Spoon filling into potato skin. Top with remaining Cheddar and sprinkle with paprika. Bake 20–25 minutes until cheese is melted and starting to bubble. Cool 5 minutes.

8. Garnish with remaining 1 tablespoon green onion and serve.

VEGETABLE LOVER'S PIZZA

PREP TIME: 10 MINUTES | COOK TIME: 13 MINUTES | SERVES 1

 Ready-to-bake pizza crust makes pizza night at home faster than ordering delivery! This pizza is a great place to use up those vegetable scraps, so plan for this toward the end of the week on your meal plan.

INGREDIENTS

1 (8") ready-to-bake pizza crust

¼ cup canned crushed tomatoes, undrained

1 teaspoon tomato paste

¼ teaspoon dried oregano

⅛ teaspoon ground fennel

⅛ teaspoon garlic powder

⅓ cup shredded mozzarella cheese

¼ cup thinly sliced yellow onion

¼ cup thinly sliced red bell pepper

⅓ cup sliced button mushrooms

2 tablespoons chopped drained marinated artichoke hearts

2 tablespoons sliced black olives

1 tablespoon grated Parmesan cheese

⅛ teaspoon crushed red pepper flakes

1. Preheat oven to 400°F.

2. Bake pizza crust on oven rack 3 minutes. Remove from oven and transfer to a sheet pan lined with baking parchment.

3. While crust bakes, add crushed tomatoes, tomato paste, oregano, fennel, and garlic powder to a small bowl and mix well.

4. Spread top of warmed crust with tomato sauce. Top with mozzarella, then layer on onion, bell pepper, mushrooms, artichokes, and olives. Bake 8–10 minutes until cheese is melted and vegetables are tender.

5. Remove pizza from oven and top with Parmesan and red pepper flakes. Cool 3 minutes before serving.

Make It with Fresh Dough

To use store-bought fresh pizza dough, use ¼ of dough ball. Let stand at room temperature for 20 minutes, then stretch into an 8" round and bake on a parchment-lined sheet pan for 5 minutes. Remove from oven, add your sauce and toppings, and return to the oven for 10–12 minutes, until cheese is melted and toppings are hot.

PER SERVING

Calories: 592 | Fat: 15g | Protein: 24g | Sodium: 1,570mg | Fiber: 7g
Carbohydrates: 88g | Sugar: 10g

HERBED COUSCOUS-STUFFED ZUCCHINI

PREP TIME: 20 MINUTES | COOK TIME: 30 MINUTES | SERVES 1

 This summery dish is the perfect way to enjoy zucchini when it is in season. It's also ready in a flash, so it can be included any night of the week on your meal plan! For added richness, drizzle with ½ teaspoon extra-virgin olive oil before serving.

INGREDIENTS

⅓ cup low-sodium vegetable stock

1 teaspoon salted butter

3 tablespoons uncooked couscous

¼ teaspoon freeze-dried chives

⅛ teaspoon dried thyme

⅛ teaspoon onion powder

⅛ teaspoon garlic powder

⅛ teaspoon freshly cracked black pepper

1 medium zucchini, sliced in half lengthwise

2 tablespoons shredded mozzarella cheese

3 tablespoons grated Parmesan cheese, divided

1. Preheat oven to 375°F and line a ¼ sheet pan with baking parchment.

2. In a 1-quart saucepan with a lid, bring stock to a boil over medium heat. Stir in butter, couscous, chives, thyme, onion powder, garlic powder, and pepper.

3. Remove pan from heat, cover with lid, and let stand 5 minutes or until liquid is absorbed. Fluff with a fork before transferring to a medium bowl. Set aside.

4. With a spoon, scoop out zucchini seeds and discard them, leaving ¼" of flesh inside zucchini skin. Set zucchini halves aside.

5. Stir mozzarella and 2 tablespoons Parmesan into couscous until melted. Spoon couscous mixture evenly into prepared zucchini halves. Sprinkle tops with remaining 1 tablespoon Parmesan.

6. Bake 20–25 minutes until zucchini is tender and tops are golden brown. Cool 3 minutes before serving.

PER SERVING

Calories: 290   Fiber: 4g
Fat: 10g   Carbohydrates: 36g
Protein: 14g   Sugar: 6g
Sodium: 437mg

FALL ROOT VEGETABLE STEW

PREP TIME: 10 MINUTES | COOK TIME: 46 MINUTES | SERVES 2

 The second portion of this hearty stew makes an excellent lunch later in your meal plan! You can use any variety of fall root vegetables here, such as parsnips, turnips, russet potatoes, or celery root—just choose what looks best in the supermarket.

INGREDIENTS

½ cup ½" carrot pieces

1 small sweet potato, peeled and cut into ½" pieces

1 medium yellow beet, peeled and cut into ½" pieces

½ medium red onion, peeled and cut into ½" pieces

1 tablespoon olive oil

¼ teaspoon sea salt

¼ teaspoon freshly cracked black pepper

2 teaspoons vegetable oil

¼ cup chopped yellow onion

1 clove garlic, peeled and minced

2 teaspoons tomato paste

½ cup canned crushed tomatoes, undrained

1 cup low-sodium vegetable broth

½ cup drained and rinsed canned white beans

½ teaspoon Italian seasoning

PER SERVING

Calories: 315   Fiber: 10g
Fat: 11g   Carbohydrates: 45g
Protein: 9g   Sugar: 14g
Sodium: 628mg

1. Preheat oven to 400°F and line a ½ sheet pan with aluminum foil.

2. Place carrot, sweet potato, beet, and red onion on prepared sheet pan. Drizzle with olive oil, salt, and pepper and toss to coat. Bake 30–35 minutes, stirring halfway through cooking, until vegetables are fork-tender. Remove from oven and set aside.

3. In a 1-quart saucepan over medium heat, add vegetable oil. Once hot, swirl to coat bottom of pan and add yellow onion. Cook, stirring often, until tender, about 2 minutes. Add garlic and tomato paste and cook 1 minute, then stir in crushed tomatoes and broth. Bring to a boil, then reduce heat to medium-low and simmer 5 minutes or until reduced by ½.

4. Add beans and Italian seasoning to pan and stir to mix, then add roasted vegetables along with any juices on the sheet pan. Simmer 3 minutes. Serve hot.

CASSOULET WITH WHITE BEANS

PREP TIME: 10 MINUTES | COOK TIME: 29 MINUTES | SERVES 2

 This cook once, eat twice French stew is a warm and comforting recipe to add to your meal plan during the cooler months. Enjoy it with some grilled crusty sourdough bread on the side for soaking up the sauce.

INGREDIENTS

1 tablespoon olive oil

½ cup chopped white onion

½ cup chopped carrot

½ cup chopped celery

1 cup lightly packed fresh baby spinach, chopped

½ cup chopped zucchini

1 clove garlic, peeled and minced

3 medium Roma tomatoes, seeded and diced

¼ teaspoon ground fennel

⅛ teaspoon freshly cracked black pepper

2 cups low-sodium vegetable broth

1 sprig fresh rosemary

1 dried bay leaf

½ teaspoon dried thyme

1 (15-ounce) can cannellini beans, drained and rinsed

1. In a 2-quart saucepan over medium heat, add oil. Once hot, add onion, carrot, and celery and cook until tender, about 5 minutes. Add spinach and cook 3 minutes, then add zucchini and garlic and cook until garlic is fragrant, about 30 seconds.

2. Add tomato, fennel, and pepper to pot and stir well. Add broth, scraping any bits stuck to bottom of pot, then add rosemary, bay leaf, and thyme and stir well.

3. Bring mixture to a boil over medium heat, then reduce heat to medium-low, stir in beans, and let simmer 20 minutes or until liquid has reduced by ½. Remove rosemary sprig and bay leaf and serve hot. Cover and refrigerate second serving for up to 5 days.

Adding Sausage

If you want to make this a nonvegetarian dish and have a serving of smoked sausage to use up, start by slicing it and frying it in a pot over medium heat until browned. Remove from the pot and resume recipe as written, adding the sausage back in when you add the beans.

PER SERVING

Calories: 286   Fiber: 18g

Fat: 7g   Carbohydrates: 50g

Protein: 14g   Sugar: 10g

Sodium: 571mg

ASPARAGUS RISOTTO

PREP TIME: 15 MINUTES | COOK TIME: 34 MINUTES | SERVES 1

 Have the Creamy Asparagus Soup from Chapter 5 in your week's meal plan? Add this creamy and fresh risotto to your plan as well for even more delicious indulgence! Take your time while stirring the broth into the rice in this recipe to ensure that you have the creamiest result.

INGREDIENTS

2 cups low-sodium vegetable broth

1 tablespoon salted butter, divided

3 tablespoons finely chopped yellow onion

6 spears asparagus, trimmed and cut into 1" pieces

1 clove garlic, peeled and minced

⅓ cup uncooked Arborio rice

¼ cup dry white wine

3 tablespoons grated Parmesan cheese

½ teaspoon fresh lemon zest

1. In a 1-liter saucepan with a lid, heat broth over medium heat. Once broth begins to simmer, reduce heat to low and cover with lid to keep warm.

2. In an 8" skillet over medium heat, add ½ tablespoon butter. Once melted, swirl to coat bottom of pan and add onion. Cook, stirring often, until translucent, about 3 minutes.

3. Add asparagus to pan and cook 3–4 minutes until asparagus is tender. Add garlic and cook 30 seconds or until garlic is fragrant. Transfer asparagus mixture to a bowl and reserve.

4. Return skillet to heat and add remaining ½ tablespoon butter. Once melted, swirl to coat bottom of pan, then add rice. Cook until rice is starting to toast, about 5 minutes. Stir in wine and cook, stirring constantly, until wine is fully absorbed, about 1 minute.

5. Start adding hot broth to rice ½ cup at a time, stirring between each addition, until broth is almost fully absorbed, about 5 minutes between each addition and about 20 minutes total. Rice should be tender with a slight bite when it is ready. If rice is too firm, add additional water ¼ cup at a time until tender.

6. With final addition of broth, stir in asparagus mixture. Once broth is absorbed, remove risotto from heat and stir in Parmesan and lemon zest. Serve hot.

PER SERVING

Calories: 509   Fiber: 7g
Fat: 15g   Carbohydrates: 72g
Protein: 13g   Sugar: 10g
Sodium: 644mg

MUSHROOM GYRO

PREP TIME: 20 MINUTES | COOK TIME: 20 MINUTES | SERVES 1

This vegetarian gyro uses meaty mushroom strips to keep it satisfying and hearty! If you purchased your portobello mushroom for this recipe in a two pack, consider adding the Spinach and Feta–Stuffed Mushroom from this chapter to your meal plan.

INGREDIENTS

2 tablespoons plain 2% Greek yogurt

1 tablespoon grated English cucumber

¼ teaspoon fresh lemon juice

¼ teaspoon freeze-dried dill

⅛ teaspoon onion powder

⅛ teaspoon garlic powder

1 large portobello mushroom cap, cut into ½" strips

1 tablespoon olive oil

½ clove garlic, peeled and minced

¼ teaspoon dried oregano

¼ teaspoon ground cumin

⅛ teaspoon dried thyme

⅛ teaspoon freshly cracked black pepper

1 (6") pita round

¼ cup shredded iceberg lettuce

2 tablespoons diced English cucumber

2 tablespoons diced Roma tomato

1 tablespoon chopped red onion

1. In a small bowl, combine yogurt, grated cucumber, lemon juice, dill, onion powder, and garlic powder. Cover and refrigerate at least 1 hour, up to 3 days.

2. In a medium bowl, add mushroom, oil, minced garlic, oregano, cumin, thyme, and pepper. Gently toss to coat strips evenly. Cover and refrigerate 1 hour.

3. Preheat oven to 425°F and line a ¼ sheet pan with baking parchment or a silicone baking mat.

4. Spread mushroom strips evenly on prepared sheet pan. Bake 20 minutes or until mushroom is tender and golden brown around edges. During final 3 minutes of cooking, add pita to oven rack to warm.

5. To serve, place warm pita on a serving plate. Spread with yogurt sauce, then top with lettuce, diced cucumber, tomato, and red onion. Add mushroom strips, fold in half, and enjoy.

PER SERVING

Calories: 340 | Fat: 15g | Protein: 11g | Sodium: 340mg | Fiber: 4g
Carbohydrates: 43g | Sugar: 6g

PORTOBELLO MUSHROOM PARMESAN

PREP TIME: 10 MINUTES | COOK TIME: 21 MINUTES | SERVES 1

 Savory portobello mushroom is breaded and fried, then served topped with classic tomato sauce and melted Parmesan. When planning for this main dish, you can round out your plate with some cooked pasta tossed with a little extra-virgin olive oil, or serve it with Buttery Herb Rice or Roasted Asparagus with Lemon and Parmesan (both in Chapter 5).

INGREDIENTS

¼ cup canned crushed tomatoes, undrained

1 teaspoon tomato paste

½ teaspoon Italian seasoning

1 tablespoon all-purpose flour

¼ teaspoon sea salt

¼ teaspoon freshly cracked black pepper

1 large egg, beaten

3 tablespoons panko bread crumbs

1 large portobello mushroom cap

2 tablespoons vegetable oil

2 tablespoons shredded mozzarella cheese

2 tablespoons grated Parmesan cheese

1. Preheat oven to 400°F and spray a 6" baking dish with nonstick cooking spray.

2. In a small bowl, add crushed tomatoes, tomato paste, and Italian seasoning. Mix well and set aside.

3. In a small dish, add flour, salt, and pepper and mix well. To a second dish, add egg. To a third dish, add bread crumbs. Dredge mushroom cap in flour mixture, then dip into egg, then back into flour, then back into egg, then finally coat with bread crumbs. Set on a plate and let stand while heating oil.

4. In an 8" skillet over medium heat, add oil. Once oil is hot, add mushroom and fry 2–3 minutes per side until golden brown and crisp. Transfer to prepared dish top-side down.

5. Spoon prepared tomato sauce into cap. Top with mozzarella and Parmesan. Bake 10–15 minutes until cheese is melted and starting to brown. Cool 3 minutes before serving. Enjoy hot.

PER SERVING

Calories: 504
Fat: 34g
Protein: 15g
Sodium: 898mg
Fiber: 3g
Carbohydrates: 33g
Sugar: 6g

FISH AND SEAFOOD DISHES

When meal planning, you'll want to focus on foods that taste delicious, are easy to prepare, and offer a variety of health benefits so you can feel good about the meals you make. Fish and seafood definitely fit the bill since they offer a variety of flavors and textures, plus plenty of nutrition, and can be prepared in almost any method you can think of. Fish and seafood also pair well with most vegetables, grains, and starches, so they are easy to mix and match with your favorite sides and pasta dishes in your weekly meal plan.

In this chapter, you will find fish and seafood recipes ranging from fresh and light to hearty and creamy. For a lighter meal, consider making Herb-Crusted Steelhead Trout or Garlic Mussels with Grilled Bread. If you want something a little different, why not add the Baked California Roll Casserole or Coconut Curry Shrimp to your meal plan? And if you're looking for something rich and comforting, the Lobster Thermidor or Creamy Seafood Chowder have you covered. Adding these recipes to your meal plan means you'll have luscious meals to look forward to!

GARLIC SCAMPI

PREP TIME: 5 MINUTES | COOK TIME: 4 MINUTES | SERVES 1

 "Scampi," which means "large shrimp," is a yummy celebration of shrimp, butter, and garlic! Frozen shrimp, thawed in the refrigerator or under cool water, are perfect for this dish and make adding this recipe to your meal plan easy from week to week.

INGREDIENTS

2 tablespoons salted butter

1 tablespoon minced yellow onion

1 clove garlic, peeled and minced

¼ teaspoon freshly cracked black pepper

2 tablespoons dry white wine

2 tablespoons low-sodium chicken broth

8 frozen large shrimp, peeled and deveined

1 teaspoon fresh lemon juice

1 teaspoon chopped fresh parsley

1. In an 8" skillet over medium heat, add butter. Once butter is melted, add onion, garlic, and pepper and cook 30 seconds. Add wine and broth and stir well.

2. Bring mixture to a boil over medium heat, then add shrimp. Cook until shrimp are pink, opaque, and curled into C shapes, about 2–3 minutes.

3. Once shrimp are cooked, add lemon juice and stir to mix. Transfer shrimp and sauce to a serving plate and garnish with parsley. Serve immediately.

Frozen Seafood Storage

Frozen seafood has a shelf life of about 3 months if properly stored. After 3 months, your seafood has a higher risk of freezer burn, and the flavor will be less potent over time. Be sure to thaw seafood the day you plan to enjoy it to ensure freshness.

PER SERVING

Calories: 279   Fiber: 1g
Fat: 22g   Carbohydrates: 4g
Protein: 11g   Sugar: 1g
Sodium: 624mg

CREAMY SEAFOOD CHOWDER

PREP TIME: 15 MINUTES | COOK TIME: 21 MINUTES | SERVES 2

 This cook once, eat twice chowder needs nothing more to be a satisfying meal, but feel free to add some crusty bread for soaking up the last bits of chowder! The crab meat in this recipe is left over from the Baked Crab Cake with Rémoulade later in this chapter, so pair these recipes in your week's meal plan.

INGREDIENTS

1 tablespoon salted butter

¼ cup chopped yellow onion

¼ cup chopped celery

2 tablespoons finely chopped carrot

1 clove garlic, peeled and minced

¼ teaspoon Old Bay seasoning

¼ teaspoon sea salt

¼ teaspoon freshly cracked black pepper

2 tablespoons all-purpose flour

2 cups low-sodium chicken broth

1 (6-ounce) Yukon Gold potato, peeled and diced, about ½ cup

1 dried bay leaf

8 ounces cod, cubed

6 ounces frozen medium shrimp, peeled and deveined

2 ounces lump crab meat

¼ cup heavy whipping cream

¼ teaspoon hot sauce

1 tablespoon freeze-dried chives

1. In a 1-quart pot over medium heat, add butter. Once melted, swirl to coat bottom of pan, then add onion, celery, and carrot. Cook, stirring often, until tender, about 5 minutes. Add garlic, Old Bay, salt, and pepper and cook until garlic and spices are fragrant, about 30 seconds.

2. Sprinkle flour over vegetables and cook, stirring constantly, 1 minute. Slowly add broth while stirring to prevent lumps. Once smooth, add potato and bay leaf. Bring to a boil over medium heat, then reduce heat to medium-low and simmer, stirring frequently, until potato is tender, about 8 minutes.

3. Once potato is tender, add cod and shrimp. Continue to simmer until fish and shrimp are cooked through, about 5 minutes.

4. Stir in crab meat and cook 1 minute, then add cream, hot sauce, and chives. Cook 30 seconds. Remove bay leaf and serve hot.

PER SERVING

Calories: 411 | Fat: 17g | Protein: 41g | Sodium: 1,199mg | Fiber: 2g Carbohydrates: 19g | Sugar: 3g

MUSSELS IN SPICY TOMATO SAUCE

PREP TIME: 5 MINUTES | COOK TIME: 8 MINUTES | SERVES 1

 Add this recipe to your meal plan for busy days since it is ready in less than 20 minutes and requires minimal effort. Frozen mussels in the shell are best for this recipe, and they can also be added along with the shrimp to the Creamy Seafood Chowder (in this chapter) to make it extra hearty.

INGREDIENTS

2 teaspoons olive oil

2 tablespoons minced yellow onion

2 tablespoons minced celery

½ clove garlic, peeled and minced

¼ teaspoon Cajun seasoning

½ cup canned crushed tomatoes, undrained

¼ cup seafood stock

¼ teaspoon hot sauce

½ pound frozen cleaned mussels, thawed

1 teaspoon chopped fresh parsley

1 lemon wedge

1. Place a 2-quart pot that fits a steaming basket and has a lid over medium heat. Once pot is hot, add oil, onion, and celery. Cook, stirring often, until vegetables are tender, about 2 minutes. Add garlic and Cajun seasoning and cook until fragrant, about 30 seconds.

2. Add tomatoes, stock, and hot sauce to pot and stir well. Carefully place steaming basket into pot, cover with lid, increase heat to medium-high, and bring to a boil.

3. Once tomato mixture is boiling, add mussels to steaming basket and cover with lid. Steam until all mussels are opened, about 5 minutes. Discard any mussels that did not open. Transfer mussels to a bowl and pour tomato sauce over top. Garnish with parsley and juice from lemon wedge. Serve.

PER SERVING

Calories: 342   Fiber: 4g
Fat: 15g   Carbohydrates: 12g
Protein: 38g   Sugar: 6g
Sodium: 1,090mg

BAKED CRAB CAKE WITH RÉMOULADE

PREP TIME: 10 MINUTES | COOK TIME: 30 MINUTES | SERVES 1

 This filling crab cake is ready in under an hour and pairs perfectly with a fresh salad. Crab cakes can be formed and refrigerated before baking for up to 1 day, so you can prepare them the evening before you plan to serve them.

INGREDIENTS

¼ cup mayonnaise, divided

1 tablespoon whole-grain mustard

¼ teaspoon paprika

½ teaspoon Old Bay seasoning, divided

¾ teaspoon fresh lemon juice, divided

⅛ teaspoon garlic powder

2 tablespoons dried bread crumbs

1 tablespoon finely chopped yellow onion

2 teaspoons finely chopped roasted red bell pepper

⅛ teaspoon onion powder

1 (6-ounce) can lump crab meat, drained well

1. Preheat oven to 375°F and line a ¼ sheet pan with aluminum foil lightly sprayed with nonstick cooking spray.

2. In a small bowl, combine 2 tablespoons mayonnaise, mustard, paprika, ¼ teaspoon Old Bay, ¼ teaspoon lemon juice, and garlic powder. Cover and refrigerate until ready to use.

3. To a small bowl, add bread crumbs, onion, bell pepper, onion powder, remaining 2 tablespoons mayonnaise, remaining ¼ teaspoon Old Bay, and remaining ½ teaspoon lemon juice and mix well. Add crab and fold to mix. Form mixture into a patty, adding water ¼ teaspoon at a time if mixture is too dry.

4. Place crab cake onto prepared sheet pan and bake 15 minutes, then flip cake and bake 12–15 minutes more until crab cake is browned well on both sides. Cool 3 minutes before serving with sauce spooned over top.

PER SERVING

Calories: 564   Fiber: 1g

Fat: 43g   Carbohydrates: 15g

Protein: 24g   Sugar: 2g

Sodium: 1,702mg

COCONUT CURRY SHRIMP

PREP TIME: 10 MINUTES | COOK TIME: 8 MINUTES | SERVES 1

 This simple curry is terrific when you need to add a quick meal to your plan without skimping on taste. If you have it on hand, add ½ teaspoon fish sauce along with the coconut milk for an extra hit of savory flavor.

INGREDIENTS

1 tablespoon vegetable oil, divided

4 ounces frozen large shrimp, peeled and deveined, thawed

¼ teaspoon sea salt

¼ teaspoon freshly cracked black pepper

⅓ cup chopped red bell pepper

¼ cup chopped yellow onion

1 clove garlic, peeled and minced

½ teaspoon grated fresh ginger

½ teaspoon Thai red curry paste

¼ teaspoon packed light brown sugar

½ cup canned coconut milk

½ teaspoon fresh lime juice

1 tablespoon chopped fresh cilantro, divided

1. In an 8" skillet over medium heat, add 1 teaspoon oil. Once hot, swirl to coat bottom of pan, then add shrimp. Cook until shrimp are starting to curl into C shapes and are pink on one side, about 1 minute. Flip, season with salt and black pepper, and cook 30–40 seconds until shrimp are just cooked through. Remove from pan and set aside.

2. To same skillet, add remaining 2 teaspoons oil and swirl to coat bottom of pan. Add bell pepper, onion, garlic, and ginger and cook 1 minute. Add curry paste and sugar. Stir well.

3. Stir in coconut milk, scraping bottom of pan to release any brown bits. Mix until curry paste is completely incorporated with coconut milk. Let mixture come to a boil over medium heat, then reduce heat to low and simmer 4 minutes.

4. Stir in shrimp, lime juice, and 2 teaspoons cilantro. Let simmer 1 minute, then transfer to a serving bowl and garnish with remaining 1 teaspoon cilantro. Serve.

PER SERVING

Calories: 468   Fiber: 2g
Fat: 38g   Carbohydrates: 15g
Protein: 19g   Sugar: 5g
Sodium: 1,324mg

SEASONED STEAMED CRAB LEGS

PREP TIME: 5 MINUTES | COOK TIME: 15 MINUTES | SERVES 1

 When adding this meal to your plan, consider making it on your shopping day or the day after to ensure your crab legs are extra fresh. If your seafood market does not have raw crab legs, use precooked crab legs and just steam for 6 minutes. You can also swap ghee for the clarified butter.

INGREDIENTS

1 tablespoon salted butter, melted

1 clove garlic, peeled and minced

¼ teaspoon Old Bay seasoning

¼ teaspoon freshly cracked black pepper

½ pound raw snow crab legs

2 teaspoons clarified butter, melted

1 teaspoon fresh lemon juice

1. Place a 2-quart pot that fits a steaming basket and has a lid over medium heat. Add enough water to come just under steaming basket. Cover with lid and bring to a boil.

2. While water is heating, add salted butter, garlic, Old Bay, and pepper to a small bowl. Mix well, then coat crab legs in seasoning.

3. Once water is boiling, add crab legs to steamer basket. Cover with lid and steam 12–15 minutes until crab legs are thoroughly cooked and bright red.

4. In a small bowl, mix clarified butter with lemon juice. Serve crab legs hot with butter sauce on the side for dipping.

PER SERVING

Calories: 221   Fiber: 0g

Fat: 12g   Carbohydrates: 0g

Protein: 27g   Sugar: 0g

Sodium: 805mg

CRISPY FRIED SHRIMP

PREP TIME: 15 MINUTES | COOK TIME: 4 MINUTES | SERVES 1

 Soaking shrimp in a little milk for 10 minutes can help reduce any fish flavor and make the shrimp more succulent. When you include this recipe in your meal plan, consider serving it with Chopped House Salad with Ranch (Chapter 5) as a side.

INGREDIENTS

8 ounces frozen large shrimp, peeled and deveined, thawed

¼ cup whole milk

¼ cup all-purpose flour

¼ teaspoon Old Bay seasoning

¼ teaspoon sea salt

1 large egg, beaten

¼ teaspoon hot sauce

¼ cup panko bread crumbs

Vegetable oil, for frying

1 lemon wedge

1. In a medium bowl, add shrimp and milk and mix well. Cover and refrigerate 10 minutes.

2. In a small dish, combine flour, Old Bay, and salt. In a second small dish, combine egg and hot sauce. In a third small dish, add bread crumbs.

3. Drain shrimp and pat dry with a paper towel. Dredge shrimp in flour mixture, then dip in egg, letting excess drip off, then press into bread crumbs. Transfer to a plate.

4. In a 1-quart pot with high sides, add enough oil to fill pot by 1". Heat over medium heat until oil reaches 350°F. Add 4–5 shrimp at a time, frying 1 minute on each side or until shrimp are golden brown and floating.

5. Transfer shrimp to paper towel–lined plate. Spritz lemon juice over fried shrimp. Serve hot.

Creamy Tartar Sauce

A creamy dipping sauce for the shrimp is easy to whip up! In a small bowl, combine 2 tablespoons mayonnaise, 1 teaspoon dill pickle relish, ½ teaspoon freeze-dried dill, ⅛ teaspoon Worcestershire sauce, ⅛ teaspoon freshly cracked black pepper, ⅛ teaspoon onion powder, and ⅛ teaspoon garlic powder. Cover and refrigerate until you're ready to enjoy, up to 5 days.

PER SERVING

Calories: 764   Fiber: 2g

Fat: 42g   Carbohydrates: 48g

Protein: 40g   Sugar: 5g

Sodium: 1,888mg

PARCHMENT-BAKED SALMON

PREP TIME: 15 MINUTES | COOK TIME: 25 MINUTES | SERVES 1

 Baking fish in parchment keeps it tender and flavorful. You can use any meaty fish here, like steelhead trout or mahi-mahi. Pair this with Buttery Herb Rice or Roasted Broccoli (both in Chapter 5) on your meal plan.

INGREDIENTS

4 (⅛"-thick) lemon slices

1 (0.5-ounce) pack fresh dill

1 (4-ounce) salmon filet

¼ teaspoon sea salt

¼ teaspoon freshly cracked black pepper

⅛ teaspoon dried thyme

1 tablespoon salted butter

1 Preheat oven to 375°F.

2 On a 15" square piece of baking parchment, lay down 2 lemon slices and ½ of dill. Add salmon and season top with salt, pepper, and thyme. Cut butter into small pieces and dot over fish, then top with remaining 2 lemon slices and dill.

3 Bring sides of parchment on long sides of fish over top of fish and roll down toward fish, then roll sides in toward fish. Crimp all edges well to seal.

4 Transfer packet to a ¼ sheet pan. Bake 20–25 minutes until salmon reaches an internal temperature of 145°F in the thickest part of the filet. Let stand 2 minutes before carefully unwrapping and serving.

Teriyaki-Style Salmon

To make this dish teriyaki style, swap lemon, dill, and thyme for ¼ yellow onion, peeled and sliced; 1 clove garlic, peeled and minced; and 2 tablespoons teriyaki sauce. Lay onion and garlic on parchment. Top with fish, brush on teriyaki sauce, and top with butter. Bake as directed.

PER SERVING

Calories: 343

Fat: 23g

Protein: 24g

Sodium: 555mg

Fiber: 0g

Carbohydrates: 1g

Sugar: 0g

SHRIMP AND GRITS

PREP TIME: 8 MINUTES | COOK TIME: 8 MINUTES | SERVES 1

 Creamy grits and plump shrimp coated in a tangy, buttery sauce are a Southern comfort food staple. This recipe is a great place to use cream cheese and milk left over from other recipes in your meal plan.

INGREDIENTS

3 ounces frozen large shrimp, peeled and deveined, thawed

¼ teaspoon Old Bay seasoning

½ cup water

½ cup whole milk

¼ teaspoon sea salt

⅛ teaspoon onion powder

⅛ teaspoon garlic powder

⅓ cup uncooked corn grits

1 tablespoon cream cheese

¼ teaspoon freshly cracked black pepper

1 tablespoon salted butter

2 tablespoons minced yellow onion

1 clove garlic, peeled and minced

¼ teaspoon Worcestershire sauce

½ teaspoon fresh lemon juice

¼ teaspoon hot sauce

PER SERVING

Calories: 508   Fiber: 3g
Fat: 20g   Carbohydrates: 57g
Protein: 21g   Sugar: 8g
Sodium: 1,221mg

1. In a medium bowl, add shrimp and Old Bay. Toss to coat evenly. Cover and refrigerate until grits are prepared.

2. In a 1-quart pot over medium heat, add water, milk, salt, onion powder, and garlic powder. Once mixture comes to a boil, reduce heat to medium-low and whisk in grits. Cook, stirring constantly, until grits are thick and liquid is absorbed, about 5 minutes. Turn off heat and stir in cream cheese and pepper. Cover and set aside.

3. In an 8" skillet over medium heat, add butter. Once melted, swirl to coat pan, then add minced onion and garlic. Cook 1 minute, then add shrimp. Cook 1 minute, then flip shrimp and cook 30 seconds or until shrimp are curled into C shapes. Add Worcestershire sauce, lemon juice, and hot sauce. Toss to coat shrimp. Remove from heat.

4. Spoon grits onto a serving plate and top with shrimp and any sauce in pan. Serve immediately.

Grits Variations

To make your grits extra cheesy, stir in 2 tablespoons shredded sharp Cheddar with the cream cheese. To make them spicy, add ¼ teaspoon cayenne pepper into the water before boiling. To make seasoned herb grits, stir in ½ teaspoon dried herbs such as chives, Cajun seasoning, or Italian seasoning along with cream cheese.

PAN-FRIED TROUT WITH LEMON BUTTER

PREP TIME: 5 MINUTES | COOK TIME: 9 MINUTES | SERVES 1

 Elegant, easy, and fast, this is the fish dish you need on your meal plan for busy days. Pair it with Seven Layer Salad, Whipped Yukon Gold Potato with Chives, or Buttery Herb Rice (all in Chapter 5).

INGREDIENTS

1 (6-ounce) rainbow trout filet

⅛ teaspoon sea salt

⅛ teaspoon freshly cracked black pepper

1 tablespoon all-purpose flour

2 teaspoons vegetable oil

1 tablespoon salted butter

2 tablespoons dry white wine

1 tablespoon fresh lemon juice

½ teaspoon freeze-dried dill

1. Pat trout dry with a paper towel. Season both sides with salt and pepper, then coat with flour.

2. In an 8" skillet over medium heat, add oil. Once hot, swirl to coat bottom of pan, then add trout skin-side down. Cook 3 minutes, then carefully flip and cook 3–4 minutes until fish flakes easily and is golden brown. Transfer to a serving plate and tent lightly with aluminum foil.

3. Add butter to the same skillet and stir until melted. Add wine and cook, scraping bottom of pan to release any brown bits, until wine is mostly evaporated, about 1 minute. Stir in lemon juice and dill and cook 30 seconds.

4. Remove aluminum foil from plate and pour sauce over fish. Serve immediately.

PER SERVING

Calories: 428

Fat: 25g

Protein: 36g

Sodium: 338mg

Fiber: 0g

Carbohydrates: 8g

Sugar: 1g

SHRIMP PO' BOY

PREP TIME: 20 MINUTES | COOK TIME: 2 MINUTES | SERVES 1

 This New Orleans–style sandwich is made with cornmeal-crusted shrimp and dressed with rémoulade, crisp lettuce, and slices of juicy tomato. Check your grocery store bakery as they often sell single submarine sandwich, hoagie, or French bread rolls.

INGREDIENTS

2 tablespoons mayonnaise

1 tablespoon whole-grain mustard

¼ teaspoon paprika

¼ teaspoon Old Bay seasoning

¾ teaspoon fresh lemon juice, divided

⅛ teaspoon garlic powder

2 tablespoons yellow cornmeal

2 tablespoons all-purpose flour

¼ teaspoon Cajun seasoning

1 large egg, beaten

¼ teaspoon hot sauce

4 ounces frozen large shrimp, peeled and deveined, thawed

Vegetable oil, for frying

1 (6") submarine sandwich roll, split lengthwise

½ cup shredded iceberg lettuce

2 (¼"-thick) slices Roma tomato, cut in half

1. In a small bowl, combine mayonnaise, mustard, paprika, Old Bay, ¼ teaspoon lemon juice, and garlic powder. Refrigerate until ready to use, up to 3 days.

2. In a small dish, combine cornmeal, flour, and Cajun seasoning. In a separate small dish, add egg and hot sauce. Mix well.

3. Pat shrimp dry with a paper towel, then dip in egg, letting excess drip off. Dredge in cornmeal mixture. Transfer to a plate.

4. In a 1-quart pot with high sides, add enough oil to fill pot by 1". Heat over medium heat until oil reaches 350°F. Add shrimp and fry 1 minute on each side or until shrimp are golden brown and floating.

5. Transfer shrimp to a paper towel–lined plate to drain.

6. To serve, spread prepared rémoulade on both sides of roll. Lay down a bed of lettuce, top with tomato, add fried shrimp, and drizzle with remaining ½ teaspoon lemon juice. Close roll. Enjoy immediately.

PER SERVING

Calories: 888 | Fat: 54g | Protein: 34g | Sodium: 1,685mg | Fiber: 5g Carbohydrates: 67g | Sugar: 5g

HERB-CRUSTED STEELHEAD TROUT

PREP TIME: 5 MINUTES | COOK TIME: 15 MINUTES | SERVES 1

 Dried herbs are the solo meal planner's secret flavor stash! Here they are used to create a yummy crust for roasted trout filet. Enjoy this dish with a wedge of lemon and Roasted Asparagus with Lemon and Parmesan (Chapter 5).

INGREDIENTS

¼ teaspoon dried thyme

¼ teaspoon dried rosemary

¼ teaspoon freeze-dried dill

⅛ teaspoon garlic powder

⅛ teaspoon onion powder

⅛ teaspoon sea salt

⅛ teaspoon freshly cracked black pepper

1 (4-ounce) steelhead trout filet

½ teaspoon Dijon mustard

1. Heat oven to 400°F and line a ¼ sheet pan with aluminum foil lightly coated in nonstick cooking spray.

2. In a small bowl, combine thyme, rosemary, dill, garlic powder, onion powder, salt, and pepper.

3. Lightly brush non-skin side of trout with mustard. Press herb mixture over top, making sure to evenly coat. Transfer filet to prepared sheet pan and bake 10–15 minutes until fish flesh flakes easily and reaches 145°F in thickest part of filet. Let rest 3 minutes before serving.

Cook It on the Grill

Grilling adds a smokey flavor that enhances trout. To grill, heat your grill over medium heat (350°F) and lightly oil a piece of aluminum foil. Place trout skin-side down on aluminum foil and place on the grate. Close the lid and cook 3 minutes or until skin starts to crisp, then carefully flip fish and cook 4–5 minutes more until fish flakes easily and reaches 145°F in thickest part.

PER SERVING

Calories: 174   Fiber: 0g

Fat: 7g   Carbohydrates: 1g

Protein: 24g   Sugar: 0g

Sodium: 315mg

BAKED CALIFORNIA ROLL CASSEROLE

PREP TIME: 15 MINUTES | COOK TIME: 11 MINUTES | SERVES 1

 Rather than hit the sushi bar, you can save some money and enjoy the flavors of the popular California roll at home by adding this sushi-inspired dish to your meal plan. Furikake is a seasoning blend available in most grocery stores or online, but if you can't find it, feel free to leave it out.

INGREDIENTS

1 (7-ounce) package cooked short-grain rice

1 teaspoon sushi vinegar

1 teaspoon furikake

3 ounces imitation crab stick, shredded and chopped

1 tablespoon cream cheese

¼ teaspoon prepared wasabi

1 tablespoon Japanese-style mayonnaise, such as Kewpie

¼ teaspoon sriracha

12 (¹⁄₁₆"-thick) sliced rounds of English cucumber

6 sheets nori

1. Preheat broiler to 500°F and lightly spray a 6" baking dish with nonstick cooking spray.

2. Add rice to a small microwave-safe bowl and microwave on high 1 minute. Add vinegar and stir to evenly coat. Transfer rice to prepared dish and spread evenly into dish. Sprinkle top with furikake.

3. In a separate small bowl, add crab, cream cheese, and wasabi and mix well. Spread over rice mixture.

4. In another separate small bowl, add mayonnaise and sriracha and mix well. Transfer to a sandwich bag with one corner snipped off, then drizzle mayonnaise over crab mixture.

5. Broil 8–10 minutes until top of casserole is bubbling and starting to char lightly.

6. Remove from oven and cool 5 minutes. Serve with cucumber slices for dipping and spoon onto seaweed snacks.

PER SERVING

Calories: 566	Fiber: 1g
Fat: 16g	Carbohydrates: 87g
Protein: 19g	Sugar: 5g
Sodium: 547mg	

LOBSTER THERMIDOR

PREP TIME: 20 MINUTES | COOK TIME: 15 MINUTES | SERVES 1

 Feeling elegant? Need a dish to celebrate? Just love lobster? This recipe is for you! Lobster Thermidor is easier to prepare than you think and is ideal for lobster-loving meal planners. Pair it with Potatoes au Gratin (Chapter 5).

INGREDIENTS

1 cup water

½ teaspoon sea salt

1 (8-ounce) raw lobster tail

1 tablespoon salted butter

2 tablespoons finely chopped yellow onion

½ clove garlic, peeled and minced

2 teaspoons all-purpose flour

1 tablespoon brandy

2 tablespoons half-and-half

⅛ teaspoon dried tarragon

⅛ teaspoon freshly cracked black pepper

2 tablespoons grated Parmesan cheese, divided

1 tablespoon fine dried bread crumbs

¼ teaspoon olive oil

¼ teaspoon fresh chopped parsley

PER SERVING

Calories: 466   Fiber: 1g

Fat: 29g   Carbohydrates: 14g

Protein: 27g   Sugar: 3g

Sodium: 1,013mg

1. Line a ½ sheet pan with aluminum foil.

2. In a large pot, add water and salt. Bring to a boil over high heat, then add lobster tail and cook 7 minutes. Drain and rinse tail with cold water to stop cooking.

3. With sharp kitchen shears, cut away underside of tail shell. Remove tail meat and roughly chop. Set meat aside. Place shell on prepared sheet pan, top-side down.

4. In an 8" skillet over medium heat, add butter. Once melted and foaming, add onion and cook until soft, about 4 minutes. Add garlic and cook 30 seconds or until fragrant, then add flour and cook 30 seconds.

5. Slowly whisk brandy into skillet, then whisk in half-and-half. Simmer sauce until very thick, about 30 seconds. Remove from heat and add tarragon and pepper, then stir in 1 tablespoon Parmesan and chopped lobster meat.

6. Preheat broiler to 500°F.

7. Stuff shell with lobster mixture.

8. In a small bowl, combine bread crumbs and oil, then stir in remaining 1 tablespoon Parmesan. Top lobster tail with cheesy bread crumbs and broil until bread crumbs are golden brown, about 2 minutes. Serve immediately, garnished with parsley.

LOBSTER MACARONI AND CHEESE

PREP TIME: 15 MINUTES | COOK TIME: 32 MINUTES | SERVES 1

 Planning for a leisurely day and want something special? Add this twist on classic macaroni and cheese to your plan! If you do not have lobster on hand for this recipe, you can swap it for other cooked seafoods like crab meat or chopped shrimp.

INGREDIENTS

2 ounces dried elbow macaroni

½ teaspoon sea salt, divided

1 tablespoon salted butter

½ clove garlic, peeled and minced

1 tablespoon all-purpose flour

¼ teaspoon freshly cracked black pepper

⅛ teaspoon dried mustard powder

⅛ teaspoon Old Bay seasoning

⅔ cup whole milk

¼ cup shredded sharp Cheddar cheese

¼ cup shredded Gruyère cheese

⅛ teaspoon ground nutmeg

⅓ cup chopped cooked lobster meat

1 tablespoon crushed cracker crumbs, such as Ritz

¼ teaspoon olive oil

1. Preheat oven to 375°F and spray a 1-quart baking dish with nonstick cooking spray.

2. In a 2-quart saucepan over high heat, add water to fill pot ¾ full. Once water begins to boil, add macaroni and ¼ teaspoon salt. Cook, stirring occasionally, until pasta is just under al dente, about 8 minutes. Drain and set aside.

3. Return pot to medium heat and add butter. Once melted and foaming, add garlic and cook 30 seconds. Add remaining ¼ teaspoon salt, flour, pepper, mustard powder, and Old Bay. Whisk to combine and cook 45 seconds, then slowly whisk in milk. Cook, whisking constantly, until sauce starts to bubble and thicken, about 2 minutes.

4. Turn off heat and add Cheddar, Gruyère, and nutmeg to pot. Whisk until cheeses are melted, then fold in cooked pasta and lobster.

5. Transfer pasta to prepared dish. Mix cracker crumbs and oil in a small bowl, then sprinkle over top of pasta. Bake 15–20 minutes until edges of dish are bubbling and top is golden brown. Cool 5 minutes before enjoying.

PER SERVING

Calories: 768 | Fat: 35g | Protein: 44g | Sodium: 1,587mg | Fiber: 3g
Carbohydrates: 61g | Sugar: 10g

MISO-GLAZED SALMON

PREP TIME: 5 MINUTES | COOK TIME: 12 MINUTES | SERVES 1

 Miso adds a super savory flavor to this salmon dish, and the glaze can also be used on shrimp, chicken, or other fish filets. This dish goes perfectly with sides like Buttery Herb Rice or Honey-Glazed Carrots (both in Chapter 5).

INGREDIENTS

½ teaspoon white miso paste

¼ teaspoon light soy sauce

¼ teaspoon honey

¼ teaspoon olive oil

⅛ teaspoon fresh lemon juice

⅛ teaspoon freshly cracked black pepper

1 (4-ounce) salmon filet

½ teaspoon toasted sesame seeds

1 teaspoon thinly sliced green onion, green part only

1. Heat oven to 375°F and line a small baking sheet with aluminum foil lightly coated in nonstick cooking spray.

2. In a small bowl, combine miso paste, soy sauce, honey, oil, lemon juice, and pepper.

3. Lightly brush top of salmon with miso mixture on all sides. Transfer filet to prepared baking sheet and bake for 10–12 minutes, until fish flesh flakes easily and reaches 145°F in thickest part of filet.

4. Remove from oven and garnish with sesame seeds and green onion. Serve immediately.

PER SERVING

Calories: 262   Fiber: 0g

Fat: 14g   Carbohydrates: 3g

Protein: 24g   Sugar: 2g

Sodium: 255mg

GARLIC MUSSELS WITH GRILLED BREAD

PREP TIME: 15 MINUTES | COOK TIME: 17 MINUTES | SERVES 1

 This dish needs nothing to make it complete, but you can certainly pair it with a glass of wine or a side of pasta dressed with olive oil and garlic. If you do not like to cook with wine, just swap it with chicken broth.

INGREDIENTS

2 (¼"-thick) slices ciabatta bread

½ teaspoon extra-virgin olive oil

1 tablespoon salted butter

2 tablespoons minced yellow onion

1 clove garlic, peeled and minced

¼ teaspoon Italian seasoning

¼ cup dry white wine

¼ teaspoon hot sauce

½ pound frozen cleaned mussels, thawed

1 teaspoon chopped fresh parsley

1 lemon wedge

1. Brush both sides of bread slices with oil. Heat a grill pan over medium heat. Once hot, add bread and grill 2–3 minutes per side until bread has golden-brown grill marks. Set aside.

2. Place a 2-quart pot that fits a steaming basket and has a lid over medium heat. Once pot is hot, add butter. Once melted, swirl to coat pan, then add onion. Cook, stirring often, until tender, about 2 minutes. Add garlic and Italian seasoning and cook until fragrant, about 30 seconds.

3. Add wine and hot sauce to pot and stir well. Carefully place steaming basket into pot, cover with lid, and bring sauce to a boil.

4. Once boiling, add mussels to pot and cover with lid. Steam until all mussels are opened, about 5 minutes. Discard any mussels that did not open. Transfer mussels to a serving bowl.

5. Increase heat to high and boil sauce until it reduces by ½, about 3 minutes. Pour over mussels. Garnish with parsley and juice from lemon wedge and serve with prepared bead.

PER SERVING

Calories: 501   Fiber: 3g
Fat: 18g   Carbohydrates: 48g
Protein: 30g   Sugar: 2g
Sodium: 887mg

CHAPTER 9
MEAT AND POULTRY DISHES

Meat and poultry dishes offer a lot of meal planning benefits for the solo cook. First, they are filling, flavorful, and packed with protein, so they are sure to keep you satisfied. Second, meat and poultry dishes offer more opportunities to cook once and eat twice, so you can have a second serving ready to heat up and enjoy later in the week when time is tight. Finally, meat and poultry can be purchased in portions for one at your butcher's counter, or purchased in larger portions that can be frozen in single servings, helping you reduce waste!

In this chapter, you will find poultry, pork, and beef dishes for all seasons and tastes. If you are looking for a fun meal, try the Baked Cheeseburger Sliders or Karaage (Japanese Fried Chicken). When you need a dish to warm up both your body and soul, add the Chicken Potpie or Barbecue-Glazed Meatloaf to your meal plan. Looking for something sweet and savory? Honey Mustard–Roasted Chicken Legs and Peach-Glazed Pork Chop are ready in under an hour! With these recipes, you will be set up for a week of delicious eating!

PEACH-GLAZED PORK CHOP

PREP TIME: 8 MINUTES | COOK TIME: 19 MINUTES | SERVES 2

 Fresh peaches and apricot jam make a sticky glaze for these chops, which are perfect with Macaroni Salad or Traditional Potato Salad (both in Chapter 5) or a simple side salad. The second serving is best heated in the oven, but in a pinch it can be heated for 1 minute on high in the microwave.

INGREDIENTS

¼ cup apricot jam

½ cup fresh peach slices

1 tablespoon brandy

¼ teaspoon onion powder

¼ teaspoon dried thyme

2 (6-ounce) boneless pork chops

¼ teaspoon sea salt

¼ teaspoon freshly cracked black pepper

1 tablespoon vegetable oil

2 tablespoons dry white wine

1. In a 1-quart saucepan, add jam, peach, brandy, onion powder, and thyme. Heat over low heat and cook, stirring constantly, until mixture starts to simmer, about 6 minutes. Continue to cook, stirring constantly, until peaches soften and start to break down, about 4 minutes. Turn off heat and set aside.

2. Season pork chops with salt and pepper on both sides.

3. Heat an 8" skillet over medium heat. Once hot, add oil and swirl to coat bottom of pan. Add chops and cook 2 minutes. Flip and cook another 2 minutes or until chops reach an internal temperature of 140°F.

4. Remove chops from skillet and add wine to skillet, scraping any brown bits from bottom. Add prepared glaze and let come to a simmer, about 2 minutes, then add chops, turn to coat, and let cook 2–3 minutes while turning frequently until chops are thickly glazed. Serve first chop immediately.

5. Wrap second chop tightly in aluminum foil. When ready to reheat, bake wrapped chop in a 350°F oven for 10 minutes.

PER SERVING

Calories: 418   Fiber: 1g

Fat: 14g   Carbohydrates: 30g

Protein: 41g   Sugar: 21g

Sodium: 635mg

SEARED BEEF FILET WITH HERB BUTTER

PREP TIME: 5 MINUTES | COOK TIME: 8 MINUTES | SERVES 1

 A tender filet mignon is an elegant dinner that makes you feel special. When adding this main dish to your meal plan, consider pairing it with the Whipped Yukon Gold Potato with Chives or Honey-Glazed Carrots (both in Chapter 5).

INGREDIENTS

2 tablespoons salted butter, at room temperature

¼ teaspoon dried thyme

¼ teaspoon dried rosemary

¼ teaspoon dried oregano

1 (8-ounce) filet mignon

¼ teaspoon vegetable oil

¼ teaspoon sea salt

¼ teaspoon freshly cracked black pepper

1. In a small bowl, add butter, thyme, rosemary, and oregano. Mix well and let stand 5 minutes or cover and refrigerate up to 5 days.

2. Heat a cast iron skillet over high heat. Once skillet starts to smoke, reduce heat to medium-high.

3. Lightly brush filet mignon with oil. Season on all sides with salt and pepper. Place filet into skillet and cook without moving 2 minutes.

4. Flip filet and add herb butter to skillet. Cook, spooning butter as it melts over top of filet, until it reaches your preferred level of doneness—an additional 3 minutes for rare, 4 minutes for medium, 5 minutes for medium-well, and 6 minutes for well-done.

5. Once cooked to your liking, transfer filet to a serving plate and spoon butter from pan over top. Let rest 2 minutes before enjoying.

Quick Peppercorn Pan Sauce

To make a scrumptious peppercorn pan sauce for your filet, remove the steak from the skillet and return the skillet to medium heat. Add 1 tablespoon brandy and 3 tablespoons beef broth and scrape any bits from the bottom of the pan. Reduce heat to low and add ½ teaspoon lightly crushed whole peppercorns and 1 tablespoon heavy whipping cream. Simmer, about 30 seconds, and enjoy!

PER SERVING

Calories: 370
Fat: 15g
Protein: 56g
Sodium: 497mg
Fiber: 0g
Carbohydrates: 1g
Sugar: 0g

HONEY MUSTARD–ROASTED CHICKEN LEGS

PREP TIME: 5 MINUTES | COOK TIME: 22 MINUTES | SERVES 1

 You can marinate these chicken legs up to 2 days ahead of time to save time the day you are cooking. If you would like to double this recipe, you can enjoy these chicken legs cold or at room temperature, or shred the meat for sandwiches.

INGREDIENTS

2 (4-ounce) chicken legs

2 tablespoons Dijon mustard

1 tablespoon honey

¼ teaspoon sea salt

¼ teaspoon freshly cracked black pepper

⅛ teaspoon ground cinnamon

⅛ teaspoon dried thyme

1. In a medium bowl, combine chicken, mustard, honey, salt, pepper, cinnamon, and thyme. Cover and refrigerate 30 minutes, up to 2 days.

2. Preheat oven to 425°F and line a ½ sheet pan with aluminum foil lightly sprayed with nonstick cooking spray.

3. Place chicken on prepared sheet pan. Bake 10 minutes, flip, and bake another 10–12 minutes until legs are golden brown and reach an internal temperature of 165°F. Remove from oven and let cool 3 minutes before enjoying.

Chicken Wings Variation

Want to make wings instead of legs? Rather than marinate the chicken, mix the sauce and set it aside. Bake wings at 425°F on a baking rack set over a sheet pan for 20 minutes, do not flip, then toss in the prepared sauce. For extra-crispy wings, let wings sit uncovered on a rack in the refrigerator for up to 12 hours before baking.

PER SERVING

Calories: 458   Fiber: 0g

Fat: 17g   Carbohydrates: 20g

Protein: 46g   Sugar: 17g

Sodium: 1,318mg

BEEF AND PORK MEATBALLS

PREP TIME: 10 MINUTES | COOK TIME: 14 MINUTES | SERVES 2

 This is a cook once, eat twice main dish, so you can enjoy savory meatballs twice in one week or freeze the second portion for the following week. Try simmering them in tomato sauce after baking to pair with pasta or make meatball sandwiches.

INGREDIENTS

⅓ cup panko bread crumbs

2 tablespoons whole milk

6 ounces 90/10 ground beef

6 ounces ground pork

1 large egg yolk

2 tablespoons grated
Parmesan cheese

1 clove garlic, peeled and
finely minced

½ teaspoon onion powder

½ teaspoon Italian seasoning

¼ teaspoon sea salt

¼ teaspoon freshly cracked
black pepper

1. In a small bowl, add bread crumbs and milk. Stir well and let stand 5 minutes.

2. In a medium bowl, add remaining ingredients and bread crumb mixture. Mix with hands until everything is just combined. Do not overmix. Cover bowl and refrigerate 1 hour.

3. Preheat oven to 400°F and line a ½ sheet pan with aluminum foil lightly sprayed with nonstick cooking spray.

4. Divide and form meat mixture into twelve balls. Place 1" apart on prepared sheet pan. Bake 12–14 minutes until meatballs are golden brown and reach an internal temperature of 160°F. Transfer to a paper towel–lined plate and cool 1 minute before enjoying.

5. Refrigerate second portion of meatballs in an airtight container for up to 5 days. Reheat second portion in a 350°F oven 10 minutes, or microwave on high 2 minutes.

PER SERVING

Calories: 361   Fiber: 0g

Fat: 13g   Carbohydrates: 15g

Protein: 39g   Sugar: 1g

Sodium: 428mg

BRAISED BEEF SHORT RIB

PREP TIME: 10 MINUTES | COOK TIME: 1 HOUR 51 MINUTES | SERVES 1

 Beef short ribs take a bit of time to simmer, but the resulting meat is buttery, soft, and melt-in-your-mouth tender. This dish is perfect alongside Whipped Yukon Gold Potato with Chives (Chapter 5), so be sure to add it to your plan for the week!

INGREDIENTS

1 (8-ounce) bone-in English beef short rib

⅛ teaspoon Montreal steak seasoning

1 teaspoon olive oil

¼ cup roughly chopped yellow onion

½ teaspoon tomato paste

½ clove garlic, peeled and minced

1 cup low-sodium beef broth

½ cup canned crushed tomatoes, undrained

1 dried bay leaf

⅛ teaspoon freshly cracked black pepper

1. Season short rib on all sides with Montreal steak seasoning. Set aside.

2. In a 2-quart pot with a lid, add oil over medium heat. Once hot, add beef and cook until browned on all sides, about 4 minutes per side. Remove beef from pot and set aside.

3. To same pot, add onion and tomato paste. Cook, stirring often, until onion is tender and tomato paste is darker in color, about 4 minutes. Add garlic and cook until very fragrant, about 1 minute.

4. Add broth to pot and stir, scraping any bits from bottom of pot. Add crushed tomatoes, bay leaf, and pepper. Stir well.

5. Bring mixture to a boil. Once boiling, return beef to pot, reduce heat to medium-low, cover, and simmer 1½ hours or until beef is tender. Remove bay leaf and serve hot.

Vacuum-Sealing

To get the best value on meat, you often have to buy packs that contain enough to feed an army. Luckily, you can easily freeze meat and poultry for longer storage. If you have a vacuum sealer, you can seal individual portions for easy storage up to 6 months!

PER SERVING

Calories: 297   Fiber: 4g
Fat: 14g   Carbohydrates: 15g
Protein: 24g   Sugar: 8g
Sodium: 802mg

SWEET AND SOUR PORK

PREP TIME: 20 MINUTES | COOK TIME: 14 MINUTES | SERVES 1

 This at-home version of the Chinese takeout classic uses double-fried pork to keep it extra crunchy even after coating in sauce. Add a serving of freshly cooked white rice for a complete meal on your week's plan.

INGREDIENTS

2 tablespoons water

2 tablespoons pineapple juice

1 tablespoon ketchup

½ teaspoon rice wine vinegar

2 tablespoons plus ½ teaspoon cornstarch, divided

1 tablespoon all-purpose flour

¼ teaspoon baking powder

⅛ teaspoon Chinese five-spice powder

⅛ teaspoon ground ginger

Vegetable oil, for frying, plus 1 tablespoon extra, divided

6 ounces pork butt, cut into 1" cubes

1 large egg, beaten

¼ cup chopped red bell pepper

¼ cup chopped yellow onion

½ clove garlic, peeled and minced

PER SERVING

Calories: 817	Fiber: 2g
Fat: 55g	Carbohydrates: 38g
Protein: 37g	Sugar: 10g
Sodium: 515mg	

1. In a small bowl, whisk together water, pineapple juice, ketchup, and vinegar until smooth. Whisk in ½ teaspoon cornstarch. Set aside.

2. In a medium bowl, whisk together remaining 2 tablespoons cornstarch with flour. Add Chinese five-spice powder and ginger and whisk well.

3. In a 2-quart pot with high sides, add enough oil to fill by 1". Heat to 350°F.

4. Toss pork cubes into flour mixture and coat well, shaking off any excess flour. Dip into egg, then transfer back to flour mixture and toss to coat.

5. Carefully transfer five or six pork cubes at a time to hot oil and fry until golden brown, about 4 minutes. Transfer to a wire rack and fry remaining pork. Once all pork is fried, raise oil temperature to 380°F. Add all pork back to oil and fry 2 minutes or until pork is deeply golden brown and crisp. Transfer pork back to rack.

6. In an 8" skillet over medium heat, add 1 tablespoon oil. Once hot, swirl to coat bottom of pan, then add bell pepper and onion. Cook 3 minutes, then add garlic and cook 30 seconds. Whisk prepared sauce and add to pan to cook until it starts to boil and thicken, about 30 seconds. Add cooked pork and toss to coat evenly in sauce. Serve immediately.

PORK EGG ROLL IN A BOWL

PREP TIME: 10 MINUTES | COOK TIME: 11 MINUTES | SERVES 1

 Looking for a quick and tasty way to use up extra ground pork from the Beef and Pork Meatballs (in this chapter)? This recipe uses ground pork along with coleslaw mix, which is used in the Soba Noodles with Peanut Sauce (Chapter 6), to make a one-bowl meal you will love!

INGREDIENTS

1 tablespoon vegetable oil

2 tablespoons chopped yellow onion

½ clove garlic, peeled and minced

3 ounces ground pork

1 tablespoon hoisin sauce

1 teaspoon oyster sauce

½ teaspoon white miso paste

1 cup bagged coleslaw mix

2 teaspoons light soy sauce

2 tablespoons thinly sliced green onion, green part only

¼ teaspoon toasted sesame oil

1. In an 8" skillet over medium-high heat, add vegetable oil. Once hot, swirl to coat bottom of pan, then add onion. Cook 30 seconds, then add garlic and cook 1 minute. Add pork and cook, crumbling well, until no longer pink, about 3 minutes.

2. Add hoisin sauce, oyster sauce, and miso paste to skillet. Mix until pork is evenly coated, then cook 1 minute. Stir in coleslaw mix and soy sauce and cook until coleslaw is just starting to become soft, about 2 minutes. If you prefer your cabbage very soft, cook an additional 2–3 minutes to desired doneness.

3. Transfer to a serving bowl. Garnish with green onion and drizzle with sesame oil. Serve immediately.

Make It with Chicken

To make chicken egg roll in a bowl, swap the pork for 4 ounces boneless, skinless chicken breast cut into ½" cubes. Add to the skillet after you cook the onion and garlic, and brown it on all sides, about 1 minute per side. Then proceed with the recipe as directed.

PER SERVING

Calories: 324
Fat: 18g
Protein: 21g
Sodium: 1,188mg

Fiber: 3g
Carbohydrates: 17g
Sugar: 9g

CHICKEN AND GREEN CHILI STACKED ENCHILADAS

PREP TIME: 10 MINUTES | COOK TIME: 27 MINUTES | SERVES 1

 Stacked enchiladas are easy to make, perfect for a solo cook, and ideal for busy days on your meal plan. You can prepare these enchiladas up to the point of baking and refrigerate for up to 3 days before finishing in the oven, adding an extra 2 minutes to the cooking time, and enjoying.

INGREDIENTS

½ cup shredded cooked chicken breast

⅓ cup shredded sharp Cheddar cheese, divided

¼ cup frozen corn kernels, thawed

¼ cup drained and rinsed canned black beans

2 tablespoons sour cream

¼ cup prepared green chili enchilada sauce

3 (6") yellow corn tortillas

1. Preheat oven to 375°F and spray a 6" baking dish with nonstick cooking spray.

2. In a medium bowl, combine chicken, ¼ cup Cheddar, corn, beans, and sour cream. Set aside.

3. In prepared dish, add 1 tablespoon enchilada sauce. Top with 1 tortilla, then ½ of chicken mixture. Drizzle 1 tablespoon sauce over chicken mixture, top with another tortilla, then add remaining chicken mixture. Drizzle with 1 tablespoon sauce, then top with last tortilla. Spread remaining 1 tablespoon sauce over top tortilla and sprinkle with remaining Cheddar.

4. Cover dish tightly with aluminum foil and bake 15 minutes, then uncover and bake 10–12 minutes until cheese is melted and bubbling and just starting to brown. Remove from oven and cool 3 minutes before enjoying.

Green Chili Enchilada Sauce Uses

Want to use up your extra green chili enchilada sauce? Try these options! Spoon 2–3 tablespoons over scrambled eggs, add 2 tablespoons to your Baked Macaroni and Cheese for One (Chapter 6), or use it as a basting sauce for baked or grilled chicken or seafood.

PER SERVING

Calories: 577   Fiber: 9g

Fat: 21g   Carbohydrates: 54g

Protein: 40g   Sugar: 3g

Sodium: 753mg

CHICKEN POTPIE

PREP TIME: 25 MINUTES | COOK TIME: 30 MINUTES | SERVES 1

 This potpie is sized just right for a solo cook, and you can make the pastry and filling up to 3 days ahead, then assemble and bake it when you're ready. You can use leftover cooked chicken here, such as rotisserie chicken or grilled chicken, if you have that on hand.

INGREDIENTS

¼ cup plus 2 teaspoons all-purpose flour, divided, plus extra for dusting

2 tablespoons salted butter, cubed and chilled

1 tablespoon ice water

2 teaspoons vegetable oil

2 ounces raw chicken breast

¼ teaspoon sea salt, divided

¼ teaspoon freshly cracked black pepper, divided

⅓ cup low-sodium chicken broth

1 tablespoon heavy whipping cream

⅓ cup frozen mixed vegetables

¼ teaspoon poultry seasoning

1. In a medium bowl, add ¼ cup flour and butter. With your fingers, work butter into flour until it resembles coarse sand with a few small pea-sized pieces.

2. Add 1 tablespoon water to flour mixture and mix with your fingers until dough starts to clump. Add additional water 1 teaspoon at a time until dough comes together and no dry flour remains.

3. Turn dough out onto a lightly floured surface and flatten dough with your palm into a flat disk about ½" thick. Fold dough in half, then press dough out again. Rotate dough a quarter turn and repeat folding and pressing twice more. Wrap dough in plastic wrap and refrigerate 30 minutes.

4. While dough chills, prepare filling. In an 8" skillet over medium heat, add oil. Once hot, swirl to coat bottom of pan, then add chicken. Season with ⅛ teaspoon each salt and pepper. Brown chicken on all sides, about 1 minute per side, until it reaches an internal temperature of 160°F. Remove from pan and set aside.

5. Sprinkle remaining 2 teaspoons flour into same skillet. Reduce heat to low and slowly stir in broth. Once mixture is smooth and starting to thicken, about 40 seconds, stir in cream. Add chicken and mixed vegetables and stir well, then add remaining ⅛ teaspoon each salt and pepper and poultry seasoning and stir to combine.

6. Preheat oven to 375°F and spray a 6-ounce ramekin with nonstick cooking spray.

7. Remove dough from refrigerator. On a lightly floured surface, roll dough out into a ⅛"-thick circle.

8. Transfer filling into prepared ramekin. Wet your finger with water and run it around edge of ramekin, then top with dough. Poke a hole in center of dough with a paring knife. Bake for 20–25 minutes until pastry is golden brown and filling is bubbling. Cool 3 minutes before enjoying.

PER SERVING

Calories: 367
Fat: 16g
Protein: 19g
Sodium: 483mg
Fiber: 4g
Carbohydrates: 37g
Sugar: 2g

KARAAGE (JAPANESE FRIED CHICKEN)

PREP TIME: 15 MINUTES | COOK TIME: 6 MINUTES | SERVES 1

 A dish traditionally served in Japanese bars with beer, this chicken is crispy and juicy with a light ginger flavor. Add this to your meal plan along with a crisp salad or the Soba Noodles with Peanut Sauce (Chapter 6).

INGREDIENTS

1 (6-ounce) boneless, skinless chicken thigh, cut into 1" chunks

1 tablespoon sake

½ teaspoon light soy sauce

⅛ teaspoon sea salt

⅛ teaspoon freshly cracked black pepper

⅛ teaspoon ground ginger

½ clove garlic, peeled and grated

2 tablespoons cornstarch

1 tablespoon all-purpose flour

Vegetable oil, for frying

1 lemon wedge

1 tablespoon Japanese-style mayonnaise, such as Kewpie

1. In a medium bowl, combine chicken, sake, soy sauce, salt, pepper, ginger, and garlic. Cover and refrigerate 20 minutes.

2. In a small bowl, combine cornstarch and flour. Set aside.

3. In a 2-quart pot with high sides, add enough oil to fill by 1". Heat to 350°F.

4. Dredge chicken pieces in cornstarch mixture, then add to hot oil 5 or 6 pieces at a time. Cook until chicken is golden brown and floating, about 2 minutes. Transfer to a wire rack.

5. To serve, spritz chicken with lemon and dip into mayonnaise. Serve hot.

Miso Salad Dressing

A green salad is the perfect side for Karaage, and you can make a simple dressing by combining 2 teaspoons vegetable oil, 1 teaspoon white miso paste, 1 teaspoon rice wine vinegar, ¼ teaspoon light soy sauce, ⅛ teaspoon granulated sugar, and ⅛ teaspoon toasted sesame seeds. Mix well and toss with 3 cups salad greens.

PER SERVING

Calories: 567   Fiber: 1g

Fat: 35g   Carbohydrates: 22g

Protein: 33g   Sugar: 0g

Sodium: 480mg

GROUND BEEF CHILI

PREP TIME: 15 MINUTES | COOK TIME: 50 MINUTES | SERVES 2

This easy chili is sure to become a go-to recipe for cooler weather, for when you're watching your favorite sports game, or for enjoying anytime you want a spicy bowl of comfort food. The leftover portion stays fresh for up to 5 days in the refrigerator or can be frozen for up to 1 month.

INGREDIENTS

1 teaspoon vegetable oil

½ medium yellow onion, peeled and chopped

1 clove garlic, peeled and minced

½ pound 90/10 ground beef

½ teaspoon sea salt

½ teaspoon freshly cracked black pepper

2 tablespoons chili powder

1 chipotle pepper in adobo, minced

1 teaspoon ground cumin

½ teaspoon smoked paprika

3 cups low-sodium beef broth

¼ cup shredded sharp Cheddar cheese, divided

¼ cup sour cream, divided

1. In a 2-quart pot with a lid, add oil over medium heat. Once hot, swirl to coat bottom of pot, then add onion. Cook 3 minutes, then add garlic and cook 30 seconds.

2. Add beef, salt, and pepper to pot and cook, crumbling well, until beef is browned, about 5 minutes. Stir in chili powder, chipotle pepper, cumin, and paprika and cook 1 minute or until spices are very fragrant.

3. Stir broth into pot, scraping bottom of pot to release any browned bits. Bring mixture to a boil over medium heat, then reduce heat to low, cover, and cook 30 minutes.

4. Remove lid and stir chili well. Raise heat to medium-low and continue to simmer until chili is thick, 8–10 minutes.

5. Serve chili topped with 2 tablespoons Cheddar and sour cream per serving.

Chili Serving Options

To make a Frito pie, top 1 ounce Fritos corn chips with ½ serving of prepared Ground Beef Chili, ¼ cup shredded sharp Cheddar cheese, and 1 tablespoon minced yellow onion. For a chili dog, top a hot dog in a bun with 2 tablespoons prepared Ground Beef Chili and 2 tablespoons shredded sharp Cheddar cheese.

PER SERVING

Calories: 390	Fiber: 5g
Fat: 21g	Carbohydrates: 12g
Protein: 34g	Sugar: 5g
Sodium: 1,492mg	

CHICKEN FAJITAS

PREP TIME: 5 MINUTES | COOK TIME: 13 MINUTES | SERVES 1

 When planning for these juicy fajitas in your weekly meal plan, also add the Vegetarian Charro Beans (Chapter 5) for the perfectly paired side! You can marinate the chicken for a bit longer, up to overnight, for extra flavor.

INGREDIENTS

1 (6-ounce) boneless, skinless chicken breast

1 teaspoon vegetable oil

¼ teaspoon ground cumin

¼ teaspoon chili powder

⅛ teaspoon sea salt

½ medium red bell pepper, seeded and sliced into ¼" strips

¼ medium yellow onion, peeled and sliced ¼" thick

2 (6") yellow corn tortillas, warmed

2 tablespoons sour cream

2 tablespoons shredded sharp Cheddar cheese

1. In a small bowl, add chicken, oil, cumin, chili powder, and salt. Mix until chicken is completely coated, cover, and refrigerate 20 minutes.

2. Heat a grill pan to medium heat, or your outdoor grill to 350°F.

3. Place chicken on prepared grill pan or outdoor grill and cook 4 minutes, then flip and cook 4–5 minutes until chicken is lightly charred with distinct grill marks and reaches an internal temperature of 160°F. Remove from grill and rest 5 minutes tented with aluminum foil.

4. Add bell pepper and onion to grill pan, or into a piece of aluminum foil lightly sprayed with nonstick cooking spray on outdoor grill. Cook vegetables, stirring often, until tender, about 4 minutes.

5. Slice chicken into ¼"-thick strips. Toss with grilled vegetables. Serve in warm tortillas, topped with sour cream and Cheddar.

PER SERVING

Calories: 464   Fiber: 5g
Fat: 18g   Carbohydrates: 29g
Protein: 45g   Sugar: 5g
Sodium: 403mg

CRANBERRY TURKEY MEATBALLS

PREP TIME: 15 MINUTES | COOK TIME: 25 MINUTES | SERVES 2

 These scrumptious (and festive) meatballs are awesome for the solo cook's kitchen during the holidays or anytime you want a savory and sweet meal for your plan. Ground turkey can be used in place of ground beef in any recipe that uses it in this cookbook.

INGREDIENTS

¼ cup bread crumbs

2 tablespoons whole milk

½ pound ground turkey

¼ cup finely chopped yellow onion

1 clove garlic, peeled and minced

1 teaspoon poultry seasoning

¼ teaspoon sea salt

¼ teaspoon freshly cracked black pepper

1 large egg, beaten

½ cup whole-berry cranberry sauce

2 tablespoons orange juice

½ teaspoon Dijon mustard

⅛ teaspoon ground cloves

1. In a medium bowl, add bread crumbs and milk and mix well. Let stand 5 minutes.

2. Add turkey, onion, garlic, poultry seasoning, salt, pepper, and egg to bowl with bread crumbs. Mix until well combined, then cover and refrigerate 1 hour.

3. Preheat oven to 375°F and line a ½ sheet pan with aluminum foil lightly sprayed with nonstick cooking spray.

4. Divide turkey mixture into six balls and place on prepared sheet pan. Bake 20–25 minutes until meatballs reach an internal temperature of 165°F. Remove from oven and set aside.

5. While meatballs cook, prepare sauce. In an 8" skillet over medium heat, combine cranberry sauce, orange juice, mustard, and cloves. Cook, stirring constantly, until mixture comes to a hard simmer, about 3 minutes. Reduce heat to low and let slowly simmer until meatballs come out of oven.

6. Transfer meatballs to skillet and turn to coat in sauce. Serve hot.

7. Store second serving in an airtight container in refrigerator for up to 5 days. Reheat in microwave on high for 3–5 minutes, until meatballs are steaming hot.

PER SERVING

Calories: 339   Fiber: 3g
Fat: 4g   Carbohydrates: 70g
Protein: 8g   Sugar: 56g
Sodium: 411mg

PANANG CURRY WITH CHICKEN

PREP TIME: 10 MINUTES | COOK TIME: 7 MINUTES | SERVES 1

 Panang curry has a slightly sweet red curry with a mild peanut flavor. The paste is available in Asian grocery stores and online and keeps for months in the refrigerator. Serve this with plain cooked jasmine rice (you can use the method outlined in Buttery Herb Rice in Chapter 5). No soy sauce on hand? You can swap it for fish sauce.

INGREDIENTS

1 teaspoon vegetable oil

¼ medium yellow onion, peeled and thinly sliced

½ large red bell pepper, seeded and thinly sliced

½ clove garlic, peeled and minced

1 tablespoon panang curry paste

½ cup full-fat canned coconut milk

1 (4-ounce) boneless, skinless chicken breast, sliced into ⅛"-thick slices

1 teaspoon fresh lime juice

½ teaspoon light soy sauce

½ teaspoon packed light brown sugar

1 In a 1-quart pot over medium heat, add oil. Once hot, swirl to coat bottom of pot. Add onion, bell pepper, and garlic and cook 1 minute. Add panang curry paste and coconut milk and stir to combine and melt curry paste, about 1 minute.

2 Add chicken, lime juice, soy sauce, and sugar to pot and stir well. Bring mixture to a boil, then reduce heat to medium-low and simmer until chicken is cooked through, about 5 minutes. Serve hot.

PER SERVING

Calories: 455   Fiber: 2g

Fat: 30g   Carbohydrates: 18g

Protein: 29g   Sugar: 10g

Sodium: 693mg

BAKED CHEESEBURGER SLIDERS

PREP TIME: 15 MINUTES | COOK TIME: 33 MINUTES | SERVES 1

 Four-packs of Hawaiian rolls are often available in the bakery or deli section of a grocery store, so you can buy just what you need for this recipe. When you add these sliders to your meal plan, consider serving them with Macaroni Salad or Traditional Potato Salad (both in Chapter 5).

INGREDIENTS

¼ pound 90/10 ground beef

¼ cup minced yellow onion

¼ teaspoon sea salt

¼ teaspoon freshly cracked black pepper

4 Hawaiian rolls, sliced in half horizontally

2 slices American cheese

2 teaspoons ketchup

2 teaspoons yellow mustard

2 teaspoons salted butter, melted

1. Preheat oven to 350°F and spray a ¼ sheet pan with nonstick cooking spray.

2. In an 8" skillet over medium heat, add beef. Cook, crumbling well, until starting to brown, about 3 minutes. Add onion, salt, and pepper and continue to cook until beef is well browned and onion is soft, about 5 minutes. Drain off any excess fat and set aside.

3. Place Hawaiian roll bottoms into prepared sheet pan. Top with 1 slice American cheese. Spoon meat mixture over cheese, top with ketchup and mustard, then add remaining 1 slice cheese and top halves of rolls. Brush tops with melted butter and cover pan tightly with aluminum foil.

4. Bake 15 minutes, then uncover and bake 5–10 minutes more until rolls are browned and sliders are hot throughout. Cool 3 minutes before serving.

PER SERVING

Calories: 747   Fiber: 1g
Fat: 29g   Carbohydrates: 76g
Protein: 43g   Sugar: 27g
Sodium: 1,526mg

BARBECUE-GLAZED MEATLOAF

PREP TIME: 10 MINUTES | COOK TIME: 44 MINUTES | SERVES 1

 Oats are the secret to keeping this meatloaf tender and juicy, and this recipe helps you use them up from your pantry stock. When you include this meatloaf in your meal plan, add either Potatoes au Gratin or Whipped Yukon Gold Potato with Chives (both in Chapter 5) for a side of extra comfort.

INGREDIENTS

6 ounces 90/10 ground beef

2 tablespoons rolled oats

2 tablespoons finely chopped yellow onion

1 tablespoon water

2 teaspoons tomato paste

¼ teaspoon smoked paprika

⅛ teaspoon onion powder

⅛ teaspoon garlic powder

⅛ teaspoon sea salt

⅛ teaspoon freshly cracked black pepper

3 tablespoons ketchup

½ teaspoon molasses

1 pitted Medjool date, finely chopped

¼ teaspoon Worcestershire sauce

1. In a medium bowl, add beef, oats, chopped onion, water, tomato paste, paprika, onion powder, garlic powder, salt, and pepper. Mix until well combined, then cover and refrigerate 1 hour.

2. Preheat oven to 350°F and spray a 5" × 3" mini-loaf pan with nonstick cooking spray.

3. While meat mixture chills, prepare sauce. In a small pot over low heat, add ketchup, molasses, date, and Worcestershire sauce. Cook, stirring often, until mixture starts to simmer, about 2 minutes. Cook 2 minutes more or until thick enough to coat the back of a spoon. Set aside.

4. Press beef mixture into prepared pan. Bake 15 minutes, then remove from oven and spoon prepared sauce over top of meatloaf. Return to oven and bake 20–25 minutes until meatloaf reaches an internal temperature of 165°F.

5. Remove pan from oven and let stand 10 minutes before serving.

PER SERVING

Calories: 464

Fat: 13g

Protein: 38g

Sodium: 862mg

Fiber: 4g

Carbohydrates: 47g

Sugar: 32g

BEEF SHORT RIB POT ROAST

PREP TIME: 15 MINUTES | COOK TIME: 2 HOURS 55 MINUTES | SERVES 2

 This comforting pot roast is perfect with some crusty bread for soaking up the juices! If you have the Braised Beef Short Rib from this chapter on your meal plan and have extra short ribs to use, try this recipe too.

INGREDIENTS

16 ounces bone-in English beef short ribs, bones removed

½ teaspoon sea salt

¼ teaspoon freshly cracked black pepper

2 teaspoons vegetable oil

½ cup chopped yellow onion

¼ cup chopped carrot

1 teaspoon tomato paste

1 clove garlic, peeled and minced

¼ cup dry red wine

2 cups low-sodium beef broth

1 cup baby potatoes, cut in half

¼ teaspoon dried thyme

1 dried bay leaf

1. Season all sides of short ribs with salt and pepper.

2. In a 2-quart pot with a lid, add oil over high heat. Once hot, swirl to coat bottom of pan, then add short ribs. Brown 5 minutes per side or until short ribs are deeply golden brown and crusty. Remove from pot and set aside.

3. Reduce heat to medium and add onion and carrot to pot. Cook 2 minutes, then add tomato paste and cook until tomato paste darkens slightly and is fragrant, about 1 minute. Add garlic and cook 30 seconds.

4. Stir in wine, scraping bottom of pot to release any brown bits, then cook until wine is evaporated, about 1 minute. Add broth, potatoes, thyme, and bay leaf and stir well.

5. Add short ribs to pot, ensuring they are just covered by liquid, and bring to a boil over medium heat. Cover pot, reduce heat to medium-low, and simmer 2 hours.

6. After 2 hours, uncover pot and simmer 20–30 minutes until liquid has reduced and short ribs are fork-tender. Remove bay leaf and enjoy hot.

7. Store second portion in an airtight container in the refrigerator for up to 5 days. Reheat in oven set to 350°F in a small dish wrapped in aluminum foil for 20 minutes or until steamy hot.

PER SERVING

Calories: 325

Fat: 14g

Protein: 24g

Sodium: 872mg

Fiber: 3g

Carbohydrates: 20g

Sugar: 5g

Nothing is better after a delicious meal, or when you need a bit of a pick-me-up, than something sweet. However, most dessert recipes make enough to feed a small army, and that leaves you with far more than you need as a solo baker. No one wants to throw away food, and it can become boring to eat the same dessert every day for days on end. For people who love to bake, it can be challenging to find recipes that make just a serving or two. That is where meal planning for one comes to the rescue!

This chapter is packed with recipes that yield enough for 1–6 servings, with some options to prepare now and bake later. For those who love cookies and brownies, there are Freeze and Bake Snickerdoodles and Chocolate Chip Brownies. If you are craving something fruity, there are Mixed-Berry Crumble and Rustic Apple Cinnamon Tart, both perfectly portioned for one. For those looking for rich and decadent desserts, there are Molten Chocolate Cake and Crème Brûlée. No matter what sweet treat you are craving, there is something here to satisfy. When you are meal planning for one, there is always room for dessert!

FREEZE AND BAKE CHOCOLATE CHIP COOKIES

PREP TIME: 10 MINUTES | COOK TIME: 12 MINUTES | YIELDS 12 COOKIES

 There may be no better feeling in the world than knowing that hot, gooey chocolate chip cookies are just minutes away! These cookies are made to be baked from frozen, so just pull one (or two) from the freezer, bake, and enjoy. They keep for up to 3 months in the freezer.

INGREDIENTS

½ cup salted butter, at room temperature

½ cup packed light brown sugar

2 tablespoons granulated sugar

1 large egg, at room temperature

½ teaspoon pure vanilla extract

1 cup all-purpose flour

½ teaspoon baking soda

1½ cups semisweet chocolate chips

1. Line a ½ sheet pan with baking parchment. Set aside.

2. In a medium bowl, use a hand mixer to cream together butter, brown sugar, and granulated sugar until creamy, about 1 minute. Add egg and vanilla and beat until well combined, about 30 seconds. Scrape down sides of bowl as needed.

3. Add flour and baking soda to butter mixture and mix on low 10 seconds to just incorporate flour. Fold in chocolate chips with a spatula until evenly distributed and no dry flour remains.

4. Scoop batter into twelve balls and place about 3" apart on prepared sheet pan. Cover with plastic wrap and freeze 6 hours or until cookie balls are frozen solid. Transfer frozen cookie balls to a freezer bag and keep frozen until ready to use, up to 3 months.

5. To bake, preheat oven to 350°F and line a ¼ sheet pan with baking parchment.

6. Place desired number of cookie balls on prepared sheet pan and bake 10–12 minutes until cookies are golden brown around the edges and just set in the centers.

7. Cool on the pan 10 minutes before transferring to a wire rack to cool another 10 minutes. Enjoy warm or at room temperature.

PER SERVING (1 COOKIE)

Calories: 264   Fiber: 2g
Fat: 14g   Carbohydrates: 34g
Protein: 3g   Sugar: 23g
Sodium: 124mg

FRESH PEACH CUPCAKES

PREP TIME: 15 MINUTES | COOK TIME: 20 MINUTES | YIELDS 6 CUPCAKES

 These cupcakes are studded with chunks of peach and topped with a tangy cream cheese frosting. If you want to freeze these cupcakes to use in future meal plans, you can frost them before freezing; just thaw overnight in the refrigerator before enjoying.

INGREDIENTS

½ cup all-purpose flour

½ cup granulated sugar

¼ teaspoon baking powder

⅛ teaspoon baking soda

⅛ teaspoon salt

¼ cup buttermilk

1 large egg, at room temperature

1 tablespoon unsalted butter, melted and cooled, plus 2 tablespoons unsalted butter, at room temperature, divided

1 teaspoon honey

¼ teaspoon pure vanilla extract

⅛ teaspoon almond extract

¼ cup peeled and finely chopped peach (about ⅓ large peach)

1 ounce cream cheese, at room temperature

½ cup confectioners' sugar

PER SERVING (1 CUPCAKE)

Calories: 192   Fiber: 0g
Fat: 4g   Carbohydrates: 35g
Protein: 3g   Sugar: 27g
Sodium: 135mg

1. Preheat oven to 350°F and line a six-cup muffin pan with paper liners.

2. In a medium bowl, add flour, granulated sugar, baking powder, baking soda, and salt. Whisk to combine. Set aside.

3. In a small bowl, combine buttermilk, egg, melted butter, honey, vanilla, and almond extract. Pour wet ingredients into dry ingredients and use a spatula to mix until just combined, about six strokes. Add peach and fold until combined, about 4–10 strokes. Do not overmix.

4. Divide batter among prepared muffin cups. Bake 18–20 minutes until cupcakes spring back when gently pressed in the centers and tops are golden brown. Cool in pan 3 minutes, then transfer to a wire rack to cool to room temperature, about 30 minutes.

5. While cupcakes cool, prepare frosting. In a medium bowl, add cream cheese and 2 tablespoons room-temperature butter. Use a hand mixer to beat on low speed until well combined and smooth, about 1 minute. Add confectioners' sugar and beat until smooth and fluffy, about 1 minute.

6. Spread frosting over cooled cupcakes. Keep cupcakes refrigerated for up to 5 days in an airtight container until you're ready to enjoy. If frozen, cupcakes keep for up to 3 months.

MIXED-BERRY CRUMBLE

PREP TIME: 15 MINUTES | COOK TIME: 30 MINUTES | SERVES 1

 Frozen mixed berries are an ideal freezer staple for the solo cook. They can be used for topping oatmeal or yogurt, blending into smoothies, or making this sweet and tangy crumble. You can prepare this crumble 1 day ahead and refrigerate it, then bake when you are ready!

INGREDIENTS

2 tablespoons all-purpose flour

4 tablespoons granulated sugar, divided

1 tablespoon unsalted butter, cubed and chilled

1¼ cups frozen mixed berries

1 tablespoon cornstarch

¼ teaspoon pure vanilla extract

⅛ teaspoon almond extract

1. In a small bowl, combine flour and 2 tablespoons sugar. Add butter and use your fingers to rub butter into flour mixture until it forms a crumble. Cover with plastic wrap and refrigerate 30 minutes.

2. Preheat oven to 375°F and lightly spray a 6" pie dish with nonstick cooking spray.

3. In a medium bowl, combine berries, remaining 2 tablespoons sugar, cornstarch, vanilla, and almond extract. Pour mixture into prepared dish. Remove crumble from refrigerator and sprinkle evenly over top.

4. Bake 25–30 minutes until berries are bubbling and crumble is golden brown. Remove from oven and cool 1 hour before enjoying.

Apple Crumble

For an apple crumble, peel, core, and chop 1 large crisp apple, like a Granny Smith, and add it to a medium bowl with 2 tablespoons granulated sugar, 1 tablespoon cornstarch, ¼ teaspoon pure vanilla extract, and ¼ teaspoon ground cinnamon. Mix well, then transfer to prepared pie dish. Top with crumble mixture in this recipe and bake 30–35 minutes at 375°F until bubbling and brown.

PER SERVING

Calories: 459
Fat: 11g
Protein: 2g
Sodium: 1mg

Fiber: 5g
Carbohydrates: 88g
Sugar: 61g

NO-BAKE CHEESECAKE WITH BERRY SAUCE

PREP TIME: 15 MINUTES | COOK TIME: 6 MINUTES | SERVES 1

This mousse-like no-bake cheesecake has a light lemon flavor that pairs scrumptiously with the mixed berry sauce. You can make this treat up to 5 days before eating if you have time to get ahead on your meal plan for the week; the flavor improves the longer it sits! Top with the sauce just before serving.

INGREDIENTS

1 ounce cream cheese, at room temperature

2 tablespoons confectioners' sugar, divided

¼ cup heavy whipping cream

½ teaspoon fresh lemon zest

¼ teaspoon pure vanilla extract

¼ cup frozen mixed berries, thawed

2 teaspoons granulated sugar

1. In a medium bowl, add cream cheese and 1 tablespoon confectioners' sugar. Beat on low speed with a hand mixer 1 minute, then increase speed to medium and whip until fluffy, about 2 minutes. Scrape down sides of bowl and set aside.

2. In a separate medium bowl, add cream, lemon zest, vanilla, and remaining 1 tablespoon confectioners' sugar. Beat on medium speed until cream forms soft peaks, about 1 minute.

3. Transfer cream to cream cheese mixture and beat on low speed until well mixed, then increase speed to high and beat 30 seconds. Scrape down sides of bowl, cover, and refrigerate 2 hours.

4. While mixture chills, prepare berry sauce. In a small saucepan over medium-low heat, add berries and granulated sugar. Cook, stirring constantly, until mixture comes to a boil, about 1 minute. Reduce heat to low and simmer 5 minutes or until berry mixture thickens to a syrupy consistency.

5. Transfer sauce to a small heat-safe bowl and cool to room temperature, about 20 minutes.

6. To serve, scoop cheesecake mixture into a serving bowl. Drizzle with berry sauce. Enjoy immediately.

PER SERVING

Calories: 477   Fiber: 1g
Fat: 29g   Carbohydrates: 48g
Protein: 3g   Sugar: 46g
Sodium: 125mg

LEMON BLUEBERRY POUND CAKE

PREP TIME: 10 MINUTES | COOK TIME: 30 MINUTES | SERVES 2

 If you have leftover buttermilk from making Fluffy Buttermilk Pancakes with Bourbon Maple Syrup or Blueberry Buttermilk Muffins (both in Chapter 3), you should add this sweet, blueberry-studded pound cake to your meal plan too!

INGREDIENTS

¼ cup fresh blueberries

½ cup plus 1 tablespoon all-purpose flour, divided

¼ cup granulated sugar

¼ teaspoon baking powder

⅛ teaspoon baking soda

⅛ teaspoon salt

3 tablespoons buttermilk

1 tablespoon plus 1 teaspoon fresh lemon juice, divided

1 large egg, at room temperature

1 tablespoon vegetable oil

1 teaspoon fresh lemon zest

¼ teaspoon pure vanilla extract

¼ cup confectioners' sugar

1 teaspoon melted unsalted butter

PER SERVING

Calories: 400 Fiber: 2g
Fat: 11g   Carbohydrates: 68g
Protein: 7g Sugar: 40g
Sodium: 320mg

1. Preheat oven to 350°F and spray a 5" × 3" mini-loaf pan with nonstick cooking spray.

2. In a small bowl, toss blueberries with 1 tablespoon flour until evenly coated. Set aside.

3. In a medium bowl, add remaining ½ cup flour, granulated sugar, baking powder, baking soda, and salt. Whisk to combine. Set aside.

4. In a separate small bowl, whisk together buttermilk, 1 tablespoon lemon juice, egg, oil, lemon zest, and vanilla. Pour wet ingredients into dry ingredients and use a spatula to mix until just combined, about five strokes. Add blueberries and fold to mix, about five strokes. Do not overmix.

5. Transfer batter to prepared pan. Bake 25–30 minutes until bread springs back when gently pressed in the center and top is golden brown. Cool in pan 5 minutes, then transfer to a wire rack to cool until just warm, about 30 minutes.

6. Once loaf is slightly warm, prepare glaze. In a separate small bowl, add confectioners' sugar, butter, and remaining 1 teaspoon lemon juice and mix until smooth. Spoon glaze over loaf, letting glaze drip down the sides. Let stand until fully cooled, about 30 minutes, before serving. Store second portion at room temperature in an airtight container for up to 3 days.

BANANA PUDDING FOR ONE

PREP TIME: 10 MINUTES | COOK TIME: 5 MINUTES | SERVES 1

 Banana pudding is a classic Southern dessert, and now you can enjoy it perfectly portioned for one! Feel free to add a few tablespoons of whipped cream to the top of this pudding before serving for extra richness. The extra banana from this recipe can be used on your meal plan for the Peanut Butter Banana Smoothie in Chapter 3.

INGREDIENTS

3 tablespoons granulated sugar

1 tablespoon all-purpose flour

¾ cup half-and-half

1 large egg yolk

¼ teaspoon pure vanilla extract

1 teaspoon unsalted butter

½ medium ripe banana, peeled and sliced

6 vanilla wafer cookies

1. In a small saucepan, combine sugar and flour. Add half-and-half and egg yolk. Whisk until smooth.

2. Heat mixture over medium-low, whisking constantly, until it just comes to a boil and thickens, about 5 minutes. Remove pan from heat and whisk in vanilla and butter.

3. Spread ⅓ of custard mixture in the bottom of an ungreased 7-ounce ramekin. Top with ½ banana slices and 3 vanilla wafers. Repeat with another ⅓ of custard and remaining bananas and wafers, ending with a layer of custard.

4. Cover and refrigerate 2 hours, up to 2 days, before enjoying.

Planning for Variety

When planning your weekly meals, be sure to plan for plenty of variety by adding new recipes each week! When you use your favorite recipes too often, they can become boring. It also helps to shop for ingredients that are in season or on sale. Variety will help keep your weekly planning more exciting!

PER SERVING

Calories: 653
Fat: 31g
Protein: 10g
Sodium: 172mg

Fiber: 2g
Carbohydrates: 82g
Sugar: 60g

CHOCOLATE CHIP BROWNIES

PREP TIME: 10 MINUTES | COOK TIME: 24 MINUTES | YIELDS 6 BROWNIES

 A little instant espresso adds a bit of richness to the chocolate flavor in these brownies. These brownies keep fresh for up to 5 days when kept in an airtight container in the refrigerator, or they can be frozen for up to 3 months.

INGREDIENTS

¼ cup salted butter, at room temperature

¼ cup packed light brown sugar

¼ cup granulated sugar

1 teaspoon instant espresso powder

1 large egg

¾ teaspoon pure vanilla extract

¼ cup all-purpose flour

3 tablespoons Dutch-processed cocoa powder

⅛ teaspoon baking powder

⅓ cup semisweet chocolate chips

1. Preheat oven to 350°F. Spray a 9" × 5" loaf pan with nonstick cooking spray.

2. In a medium bowl, use a hand mixer on medium speed to cream butter until smooth, about 30 seconds. Add brown sugar, granulated sugar, and instant espresso. Mix on medium speed until well combined, about 30 seconds. Add egg and vanilla and mix on low speed to just combine, about 10 seconds.

3. Sift flour, cocoa powder, and baking powder into bowl with sugar mixture and mix on low speed until no dry flour remains, about 20 seconds. Fold in chocolate chips.

4. Pour batter evenly into prepared pan. Bake 20–24 minutes until edges are firm and center is just set.

5. Cool in pan 20 minutes, then turn out onto a cutting board and cool 20 minutes more before slicing. Serve warm or at room temperature.

PER SERVING (1 BROWNIE)

Calories: 203　*Fiber: 2g*
Fat: 11g　*Carbohydrates: 26g*
Protein: 2g　*Sugar: 23g*
Sodium: 86mg

FREEZE AND BAKE OATMEAL COOKIES

PREP TIME: 10 MINUTES | COOK TIME: 12 MINUTES | YIELDS 12 COOKIES

 You can customize these easy oatmeal cookies by adding ½ cup raisins, candy-coated chocolates (like M&M's), or chopped nuts to the batter before scooping and freezing. Feel free to get creative with items in your pantry! The frozen cookie dough keeps for up to 3 months, so you can enjoy them for a few weeks of meal planning.

INGREDIENTS

½ cup salted butter, at room temperature

⅔ cup packed light brown sugar

1 large egg, at room temperature

½ teaspoon pure vanilla extract

1 cup all-purpose flour

½ teaspoon ground cinnamon

½ teaspoon baking powder

⅔ cup rolled oats

PER SERVING (1 COOKIE)

Calories: 175   Fiber: 1g
Fat: 8g   Carbohydrates: 23g
Protein: 2g   Sugar: 12g
Sodium: 122mg

1. Line a ½ sheet pan with baking parchment. Set aside.

2. In a medium bowl, use a hand mixer on medium speed to cream together butter and sugar until creamy, about 1 minute. Add egg and vanilla and beat until well combined, about 30 seconds. Scrape down sides of bowl as needed.

3. Add flour, cinnamon, and baking soda to butter mixture and mix on low 10 seconds to just incorporate flour. Fold in oats with a spatula until evenly distributed and no dry flour remains.

4. Scoop batter into twelve balls about 3" apart on prepared sheet pan. Cover with plastic wrap and freeze 6 hours or until cookie balls are frozen solid. Transfer frozen cookie balls to a freezer bag and keep frozen until ready to use, up to 3 months.

5. To bake, preheat oven to 350°F and line a ¼ sheet pan with baking parchment.

6. Place desired number of cookie balls on prepared sheet pan and bake 10–12 minutes until cookies are golden brown around edges and just set in centers.

7. Cool on the pan 10 minutes before transferring to a wire rack to cool another 10 minutes. Enjoy warm or at room temperature.

SPICED BREAD AND BUTTER PUDDING

PREP TIME: 20 MINUTES | COOK TIME: 34 MINUTES | SERVES 1

 This unique bread pudding has a crisp sugar topping and smooth custard with a gentle spice flavor. This recipe is an excellent place to use sandwich bread that is starting to go stale as well as leftover eggs and cream.

INGREDIENTS

2 tablespoons unsalted butter, at room temperature

3 slices white bread, crusts removed

2 large egg yolks

3 tablespoons plus 1 teaspoon granulated sugar, divided

⅛ teaspoon ground cinnamon

⅛ teaspoon ground nutmeg

½ cup heavy whipping cream

¼ teaspoon vanilla bean paste

PER SERVING

Calories: 1,118   Fiber: 3g
Fat: 74g   Carbohydrates: 90g
Protein: 16g   Sugar: 51g
Sodium: 490mg

1. Preheat oven to 350°F and spray a 6" pie dish with nonstick cooking spray.

2. Butter bread slices on both sides. Cut 1 slice into ½" cubes. Cut remaining 2 slices into four triangles each. Set aside.

3. In a small bowl, whisk together egg yolks, 3 tablespoons sugar, cinnamon, and nutmeg until smooth. Set aside.

4. In a small saucepan, add cream. Heat over medium heat until cream just comes to a simmer, about 2 minutes. Add 2 tablespoons hot cream into egg yolks and whisk well, then whisk mixture back into saucepan. Immediately remove from heat and stir in vanilla bean paste.

5. Lay cubed bread at bottom of prepared dish, then top with bread triangles. Pour custard over bread, making sure each slice is evenly coated. Let stand 10 minutes at room temperature to soak.

6. Place pie dish in a baking dish at least 2" wider than pie dish and add recently boiled water to baking dish until it reaches halfway up the sides. Bake 30 minutes or until filling is set. Remove baking dish from oven and transfer pie dish to a wire rack.

7. Sprinkle remaining 1 teaspoon sugar over top and use a torch, or broil at 500°F, until sugar is caramelized, about 2 minutes. Serve warm or at room temperature.

RUSTIC APPLE CINNAMON TART

PREP TIME: 30 MINUTES | COOK TIME: 35 MINUTES | SERVES 1

 This rustic tart is easy to put together and can be enjoyed warm with a scoop of vanilla ice cream or at room temperature with a dollop of whipped cream. When Granny Smith apples are in season or on sale at your local grocery store, you should add this recipe to your meal plan!

INGREDIENTS

½ cup all-purpose flour, plus extra for dusting

½ teaspoon granulated sugar

4 tablespoons salted butter, cubed and chilled, divided

1 tablespoon ice water, plus extra if needed

1 Granny Smith apple, peeled, cored, and thinly sliced

2 teaspoons packed light brown sugar

¼ teaspoon ground cinnamon

1. In a medium bowl, combine flour and granulated sugar.

2. Add 3 tablespoons butter to flour mixture and use your fingers to work butter into mixture until it resembles coarse sand with a few small pea-sized pieces.

3. Add 1 tablespoon water to flour mixture and mix with your fingers until dough starts to clump. If needed, add more water 1 teaspoon at a time until dough comes together and no dry flour remains.

4. Turn dough out onto a lightly floured surface and flatten dough with your palm into a fat ½"-thick disk. Fold dough in half, then press dough out again. Rotate dough a quarter turn and repeat folding and pressing twice more. Wrap dough in plastic wrap and refrigerate 30 minutes or up to overnight.

5. Preheat oven to 375°F and line a ½ sheet pan with baking parchment.

6. On a lightly floured surface, roll chilled dough into an 8" circle and transfer dough to prepared sheet pan. Shingle apple slices in circles on top of dough, starting 1½" from the edge. Fold edges of dough over apples, then sprinkle top of apples with brown sugar and cinnamon. Dot top of apples with remaining 1 tablespoon butter.

7. Bake tart 30–35 minutes until apples are tender and crust is golden brown and crisp. Remove from oven and let cool 20 minutes before enjoying.

PER SERVING

Calories: 754
Fat: 43g
Protein: 7g
Sodium: 368mg

Fiber: 4g
Carbohydrates: 80g
Sugar: 27g

CARROT CAKE

PREP TIME: 15 MINUTES | COOK TIME: 22 MINUTES | YIELDS 1 (4") ROUND LAYER CAKE

 Usually a layer cake is made to feed a crowd, but this petite version is just right for one person to enjoy over a few days. Keep the cake refrigerated in an airtight container to enjoy for up to 4 days on your meal plan!

INGREDIENTS

1 cup all-purpose flour

⅛ teaspoon salt

½ teaspoon baking powder

¾ teaspoon ground cinnamon, divided

⅛ teaspoon ground nutmeg

⅛ teaspoon ground cloves

⅔ cup granulated sugar

6 tablespoons vegetable oil

1 large egg, at room temperature

¾ teaspoon pure vanilla extract, divided

⅓ cup buttermilk, at room temperature

¼ cup finely grated carrot

¼ cup finely chopped walnuts, divided

1 ounce cream cheese, at room temperature

2 tablespoons unsalted butter, at room temperature

½ cup confectioners' sugar

PER SERVING (¼ CAKE)

Calories: 636   Fiber: 2g

Fat: 34g   Carbohydrates: 74g

Protein: 7g   Sugar: 48g

Sodium: 204mg

1. Preheat oven to 350°F and spray two 4" × 2" round cake pans with nonstick cooking spray.

2. In a medium bowl, sift together flour, salt, baking powder, ½ teaspoon cinnamon, nutmeg, and cloves.

3. In a large bowl, add granulated sugar, oil, egg, and ½ teaspoon vanilla. Use a hand mixer to blend on low speed until well combined, about 1 minute.

4. Add ⅓ flour mixture alternately with ½ buttermilk to sugar mixture, beating on low speed after each addition, ending with flour, until just combined, about 10 seconds per addition. Fold in carrot and 3 tablespoons walnuts.

5. Divide batter evenly between prepared pans. Bake 18–22 minutes until cakes spring back when gently pressed in. Cool in pans 10 minutes before turning out onto wire racks to cool to room temperature.

6. In a medium bowl, combine cream cheese and butter. Use a hand mixer to beat on low speed until well combined and smooth, about 1 minute. Add confectioners' sugar, remaining ¼ teaspoon cinnamon, and remaining ¼ teaspoon vanilla and beat until smooth and fluffy, about 1 minute.

7. To assemble, place one cooled cake layer top-side down on a large plate. Add ½ of frosting and spread in an even layer. Top with second cake layer top-side down and spread remaining frosting over top. Sprinkle top with remaining 1 tablespoon walnuts.

MOLTEN CHOCOLATE CAKE

PREP TIME: 10 MINUTES | COOK TIME: 25 MINUTES | SERVES 1

 If you love chocolate, then this recipe is a must for your meal plan! This cake can be enjoyed as it is but is also lovely with a small scoop of vanilla ice cream on the side or topped with a bit of lightly sweetened whipped cream.

INGREDIENTS

2 ounces semisweet chocolate, chopped

2 ounces salted butter, at room temperature

1 large egg, at room temperature

2 tablespoons granulated sugar

¼ teaspoon pure vanilla extract

1 tablespoon plus 1 teaspoon all-purpose flour

1. Preheat oven to 350°F. Spray an 8-ounce ramekin with nonstick cooking spray.

2. In the top of a simmering double boiler over medium-low heat, add chocolate. Stir occasionally until melted, about 3 minutes. Remove chocolate from heat and stir in butter until melted. Set aside.

3. In a medium bowl, add egg and sugar. Use a hand mixer to beat on medium speed until light and fluffy, about 1 minute. Stir in vanilla and chocolate mixture until well combined, then add flour and mix at low speed until no lumps remain, about 30 seconds.

4. Transfer batter to prepared ramekin. Bake 20–25 minutes until edges of cake are firm but center is soft when gently pressed and edges of cake are coming away from ramekin.

5. Cool cake in ramekin 1 minute before serving. You can serve directly in ramekin or on a plate. To serve on a plate, run a thin knife around edge of ramekin, place a small plate over top, flip, then carefully remove ramekin. Enjoy immediately.

PER SERVING

Calories: 961
Fat: 64g
Protein: 12g
Sodium: 441mg

Fiber: 4g
Carbohydrates: 86g
Sugar: 56g

CHEESECAKE FOR ONE

PREP TIME: 15 MINUTES | COOK TIME: 35 MINUTES | SERVES 1

 This personal cheesecake is creamy, rich, and just the right size for one! You can enjoy it the day you make it, but if you are able, try making it 1 or 2 days ahead of time so the cheesecake can really chill and set.

INGREDIENTS

¼ cup graham cracker crumbs

2 tablespoons granulated sugar, divided

1 tablespoon unsalted butter, melted and cooled

2 ounces cream cheese, at room temperature

¼ teaspoon fresh lemon zest

¼ teaspoon cornstarch

1 large egg yolk

1 tablespoon sour cream

1 teaspoon heavy whipping cream

¼ teaspoon pure vanilla extract

1. Preheat oven to 350°F and spray the bottom of a 4" springform pan with nonstick cooking spray.

2. In a small bowl, add cracker crumbs, 1 tablespoon sugar, and butter. Mix until all crumbs are well coated in butter, then transfer crumb mixture into prepared pan and press down to form a crust. Bake 8–10 minutes until crust is firm, then remove from oven and set aside.

3. In a medium bowl, add cream cheese, lemon zest, and remaining 1 tablespoon sugar. Use a hand mixer to beat on medium speed until smooth and creamy, about 2 minutes. Add cornstarch, egg yolk, and sour cream. Beat until well combined, about 30 seconds, then add cream and vanilla and mix on low speed until well incorporated, about 15 seconds.

4. Spread batter onto crust, then gently tap pan on the counter three times to level mixture. Wrap bottom of cheesecake pan with aluminum foil and place in a shallow baking dish at least 3" wider than springform pan. Fill dish with 1" of boiling water. Carefully transfer dish to oven and bake 22–25 minutes until cheesecake is set around edges but still slightly jiggly in center.

5. Carefully remove cheesecake from dish and place on a wire rack. Cool in pan to room temperature, about 40 minutes, then transfer to an airtight container and refrigerate 2 hours. Enjoy chilled or at room temperature.

PER SERVING

Calories: 600 Fiber: 1g
Fat: 38g Carbohydrates: 49g
Protein: 8g Sugar: 34g
Sodium: 340mg

CHOCOLATE CUPCAKES

PREP TIME: 20 MINUTES | COOK TIME: 18 MINUTES | YIELDS 6 CUPCAKES

 There is no better pick-me-up than a chocolate cupcake with luscious chocolate frosting. This recipe makes six cupcakes that keep in the refrigerator for up to 3 days, just right for the solo baker. You can also freeze some of the cupcakes for future meal planning; just thaw them in the refrigerator overnight before enjoying!

INGREDIENTS

½ cups all-purpose flour

¼ cup plus 2 tablespoons Dutch-processed cocoa powder, divided

½ teaspoon baking powder

¼ teaspoon baking soda

⅜ teaspoon salt, divided

½ cup granulated sugar

3 tablespoons salted butter, melted and cooled

¼ cup buttermilk

1 large egg yolk

¾ teaspoon pure vanilla extract, divided

¼ cup boiling water

4 tablespoons unsalted butter, at room temperature

1 cup confectioners' sugar

1 tablespoon whole milk

1. Preheat oven to 350°F and line a six-cup muffin pan with paper liners.

2. In a medium bowl, sift together flour, 2 tablespoons cocoa powder, baking powder, baking soda, and ¼ teaspoon salt. Set aside.

3. In a small bowl, whisk together granulated sugar, salted butter, buttermilk, egg yolk, and ½ teaspoon vanilla. Pour into flour mixture and stir until just combined. Add boiling water, stirring until smooth.

4. Divide batter among cupcake liners. Bake 16–18 minutes until cakes spring back in center when gently pressed. Cool in pans 5 minutes before turning out onto a wire rack to cool to room temperature, about 20 minutes.

5. In a medium bowl, add unsalted butter. With a hand mixer on low speed, beat until smooth. Add remaining ¼ teaspoon vanilla, confectioners' sugar, remaining ¼ cup cocoa powder, and remaining ⅛ teaspoon salt and mix on low speed until just combined, about 30 seconds. Add milk and beat on medium speed until smooth, about 1 minute.

6. To assemble, frost each cooled cupcake with chocolate frosting. Store cupcakes in the refrigerator in an airtight container for up to 3 days.

PER SERVING (1 CUPCAKE)

Calories: 316
Fat: 14g
Protein: 3g
Sodium: 299mg
Fiber: 2g
Carbohydrates: 45g
Sugar: 34g

CRÈME BRÛLÉE

PREP TIME: 20 MINUTES | COOK TIME: 56 MINUTES | SERVES 1

 Silky-smooth custard topped with crisp caramelized sugar makes a mouthwatering dessert for one. This is the perfect treat to add to your meal plan when you have extra cream and eggs that need to be used up!

INGREDIENTS

½ cup heavy whipping cream

¼ teaspoon pure vanilla extract

2 large egg yolks, at room temperature

¼ cup granulated sugar, divided

1. Preheat oven to 300°F and line the bottom of a 6" baking dish with a double layer of paper towels.

2. In a small saucepan, add cream and vanilla. Heat over medium heat until cream simmers, about 3 minutes. Set aside.

3. In a small bowl, combine egg yolks and 3 tablespoons sugar. Slowly whisk in hot cream 1 tablespoon at a time until ¼ of cream is added. Continue to whisk in remaining cream in a steady stream. Transfer mixture to a 7-ounce ramekin.

4. Place ramekin into prepared dish. Add boiled water to dish until it reaches halfway up side of ramekin.

5. Bake 45–50 minutes until custard is set around edges but still a little jiggly in center. Carefully transfer ramekin to a wire rack and cool to room temperature, about 30 minutes, then refrigerate at least 2 hours, up to 2 days.

6. To serve, sprinkle remaining 1 tablespoon sugar evenly over top of custard. With a small torch, or under a broiler preheated to 500°F, melt sugar until caramelized, 2–3 minutes. Cool 2 minutes to allow sugar to harden before enjoying.

PER SERVING

Calories: 715 Fiber: 0g
Fat: 50g Carbohydrates: 55g
Protein: 8g Sugar: 54g
Sodium: 61mg

FREEZE AND BAKE SNICKERDOODLES

PREP TIME: 10 MINUTES | COOK TIME: 12 MINUTES | YIELDS 12 COOKIES

 Life is sweet when a tray of warm snickerdoodles is just minutes away. Having a stash of this frozen dough on hand is great for the solo meal planner because these cookies can be added to your plan for weeks to come!

INGREDIENTS

⅔ cup salted butter

⅔ cup plus 3 tablespoons granulated sugar, divided

2 tablespoons packed light brown sugar

½ teaspoon pure vanilla extract

1 large egg, at room temperature

1½ cups all-purpose flour

½ teaspoon baking soda

½ teaspoon cream of tartar

2 teaspoons ground cinnamon

1. Line a ½ sheet pan with baking parchment. Set aside.

2. In a medium bowl, use a hand mixer on medium speed to cream together butter, ⅔ cup granulated sugar, and brown sugar until creamy, about 1 minute. Add vanilla and egg and beat until well combined, about 30 seconds. Scrape down sides of bowl as needed.

3. Add flour, baking soda, and cream of tartar to butter mixture and mix on low 10 seconds to just incorporate flour, then increase speed to medium and beat until batter is smooth, about 30 seconds.

4. In a small bowl, combine remaining 3 tablespoons granulated sugar and cinnamon.

5. Scoop batter into twelve balls and roll in cinnamon-sugar mixture. Place on prepared sheet pan about 1" apart and gently flatten each ball to ½" thickness. Cover with plastic wrap and freeze 6 hours or until cookies are frozen solid. Transfer frozen cookies to a freezer bag and keep frozen until ready to use.

6. To bake, preheat oven to 350°F and line a ¼ sheet pan with baking parchment. Place desired number of cookie balls on prepared sheet pan and bake 10–12 minutes until cookies are just starting to turn golden brown around edges.

7. Cool on the pan 10 minutes before transferring to a wire rack to cool another 10 minutes. Enjoy warm or at room temperature.

PER SERVING (1 COOKIE)

Calories: 218 Fiber: 1g
Fat: 10g Carbohydrates: 29g
Protein: 2g Sugar: 17g
Sodium: 140mg

PECAN BLONDIES

PREP TIME: 10 MINUTES | COOK TIME: 24 MINUTES | YIELDS 6 BLONDIES

 Brown sugar gives these buttery blondies a mild caramel flavor that enhances the chopped pecans. You can swap the pecans in this recipe for any chopped nuts you have on hand in your pantry. Peanuts, walnuts, and almonds are all good alternatives. You can also swap them for white chocolate, butterscotch, or chocolate chips too!

INGREDIENTS

¼ cup salted butter, at room temperature

⅓ cup packed light brown sugar

2 tablespoons granulated sugar

1 large egg yolk

¾ teaspoon pure vanilla extract

⅛ teaspoon almond extract

½ cup all-purpose flour

⅛ teaspoon baking powder

⅓ cup chopped roasted, unsalted pecans

1. Preheat oven to 350°F and spray a 9" × 5" loaf pan with nonstick cooking spray.

2. In a medium bowl, use a hand mixer on medium speed to cream butter until smooth, about 30 seconds. Add brown sugar and granulated sugar and mix on medium speed until well combined, about 30 seconds. Add egg yolk, vanilla, and almond extract and mix on low speed to just combine, about 10 seconds.

3. Sift flour and baking powder into butter mixture and mix on low speed until no dry flour remains, about 20 seconds. Fold in pecans.

4. Pour batter evenly into prepared pan. Bake 20–24 minutes until edges are firm and center is just set.

5. Cool in pan 20 minutes, then turn out onto a cutting board and cool 20 minutes more before slicing. Serve warm or at room temperature. Store blondies in an airtight container at room temperature for up to 4 days. The extra blondies can also be individually wrapped in plastic wrap, put in a freezer bag, and frozen for up to 3 months.

PER SERVING (1 BLONDIE)

Calories: 220   Fiber: 1g

Fat: 12g   Carbohydrates: 25g

Protein: 2g   Sugar: 16g

Sodium: 75mg

CHOCOLATE MUG CAKE

PREP TIME: 5 MINUTES | COOK TIME: 2 MINUTES | SERVES 1

 Craving a dessert on the fly or something sweet for your meal plan on a busy day? This rich Chocolate Mug Cake is just what you need. From start to finish, this cake is ready in under 10 minutes, making it a perfect (almost) instant dessert! Serve topped with a swirl of whipped cream and a sprinkle of cocoa powder for an extrasweet touch.

INGREDIENTS

3 tablespoons all-purpose flour

3 tablespoons packed light brown sugar

3 tablespoons Dutch-processed cocoa powder

⅛ teaspoon baking powder

2 tablespoons mayonnaise

2 tablespoons heavy whipping cream

1 tablespoon water

¼ teaspoon pure vanilla extract

1. In an 8-ounce microwave-safe mug, add flour, sugar, cocoa powder, and baking powder. Whisk well to combine, then add remaining ingredients and stir until mixture is smooth. Be careful not to overmix. Use a small spatula to scrape batter from edges of mug.

2. Microwave on high 1–1½ minutes until cake rises and center is firm. Let cool 30 seconds before removing from microwave and enjoying.

Why Mayonnaise?
Mayonnaise contains eggs, oil, and seasoning, which makes it the perfect one-stop ingredient for a moist and flavorful mug cake. Be sure to use full-fat mayonnaise. Reduced-fat mayonnaise has fillers and other ingredients to make it smooth that will not work to create a delicious mug cake.

PER SERVING

Calories: 570	Fiber: 7g
Fat: 33g	Carbohydrates: 69g
Protein: 7g	Sugar: 41g
Sodium: 260mg	

US/METRIC CONVERSION CHARTS

OVEN TEMP CONVERSIONS

Degrees Fahrenheit	Degrees Celsius
200 degrees F	95 degrees C
250 degrees F	120 degrees C
275 degrees F	135 degrees C
300 degrees F	150 degrees C
325 degrees F	160 degrees C
350 degrees F	180 degrees C
375 degrees F	190 degrees C
400 degrees F	205 degrees C
425 degrees F	220 degrees C
450 degrees F	230 degrees C

VOLUME CONVERSIONS

US Volume Measure	Metric Equivalent
⅛ teaspoon	0.5 milliliter
¼ teaspoon	1 milliliter
½ teaspoon	2 milliliters
1 teaspoon	5 milliliters
½ tablespoon	7 milliliters
1 tablespoon (3 teaspoons)	15 milliliters
2 tablespoons (1 fluid ounce)	30 milliliters
¼ cup (4 tablespoons)	60 milliliters
⅓ cup	90 milliliters
½ cup (4 fluid ounces)	125 milliliters
⅔ cup	160 milliliters
¾ cup (6 fluid ounces)	180 milliliters
1 cup (16 tablespoons)	250 milliliters
1 pint (2 cups)	500 milliliters
1 quart (4 cups)	1 liter (about)

WEIGHT CONVERSIONS

US Weight Measure	Metric Equivalent
½ ounce	15 grams
1 ounce	30 grams
2 ounces	60 grams
3 ounces	85 grams
¼ pound (4 ounces)	115 grams
½ pound (8 ounces)	225 grams
¾ pound (12 ounces)	340 grams
1 pound (16 ounces)	454 grams

BAKING PAN SIZES

American	Metric
8 x 1½ inch round baking pan	20 x 4 cm cake tin
9 x 1½ inch round baking pan	23 x 3.5 cm cake tin
11 x 7 x 1½ inch baking pan	28 x 18 x 4 cm baking tin
13 x 9 x 2 inch baking pan	30 x 20 x 5 cm baking tin
2 quart rectangular baking dish	30 x 20 x 3 cm baking tin
15 x 10 x 2 inch baking pan	30 x 25 x 2 cm baking tin (Swiss roll tin)
9 inch pie plate	22 x 4 or 23 x 4 cm pie plate
7 or 8 inch springform pan	18 or 20 cm springform or loose bottom cake tin
9 x 5 x 3 inch loaf pan	23 x 13 x 7 cm or 2 lb narrow loaf or pâté tin
1½ quart casserole	1.5 liter casserole
2 quart casserole	2 liter casserole

HOW TO REDUCE A RECIPE

Original Amount	Half the Amount	One-Third the Amount
1 cup	½ cup	⅓ cup
¾ cup	6 tablespoons	¼ cup
⅔ cup	⅓ cup	3 tablespoons + 1½ teaspoons
½ cup	¼ cup	2 tablespoons + 2 teaspoons
⅓ cup	2 tablespoons + 2 teaspoons	1 tablespoon + 2¼ teaspoons
¼ cup	2 tablespoons	1 tablespoon + 1 teaspoon
1 tablespoon	1½ teaspoons	1 teaspoon
1 teaspoon	½ teaspoon	¼ teaspoon
½ teaspoon	¼ teaspoon	⅛ teaspoon
¼ teaspoon	⅛ teaspoon	dash

INDEX

Note: Page numbers in **bold** indicate recipe category lists.

ABOUT THE AUTHOR

Kelly Jaggers is a cookbook author, recipe developer, and founder of the recipe blog *Evil Shenanigans* (EvilShenanigans.com). She is the author of twelve cookbooks, including *The Everything® Easy Instant Pot® Cookbook*, *The Ultimate Baking for One Cookbook*, and *The Ultimate Mediterranean Diet Cooking for One Cookbook*. Kelly is also a food stylist and photographer who has provided photography for various cookbooks and websites. When she is not busy cooking up a storm in her own kitchen, she teaches cooking classes and is a small-event caterer. Kelly lives in Dallas with her husband and two hound dogs.

COOKING SOLO
Will Never Be Boring Again!

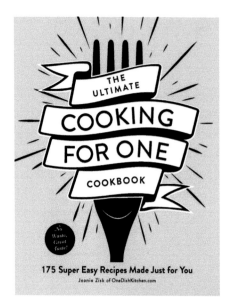

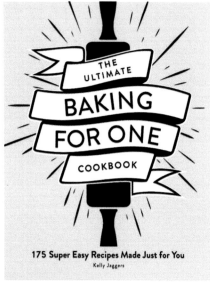

Pick up or download your copies today!